Chocolate
A Love Story

65 Chocolate Dessert Recipes
from Max Brenner's Private Collection

Chocolate
A Love Story

65 Chocolate Dessert Recipes
from Max Brenner's Private Collection

Max Brenner

Artwork by Yonatan Factor

Little, Brown and Company
New York   Boston   London

Little, Brown and Company
Hachette Book Group
237 Park Avenue, New York, NY 10017
www.hachettebookgroup.com

First Edition: November 2009

Little, Brown and Company is a division of Hachette Book Group, Inc. The Little, Brown name and logo are trademarks of Hachette Book Group, Inc.

Library of Congress Cataloging-in-Publication Data
Chocolate : a love story: 65 chocolate dessert recipes from Max Brenner's private collection / Max Brenner.—1st ed.
    p. cm.

ISBN 978-0-316-05662-5
1. Cookery (Chocolate). 2. Chocolate desserts. 3. Max Brenner (Restaurants). I. Max Brenner (Restaurants).
TX767.C5C48136 2009   2009006619
641.3'374—dc22
10 9 8 7 6 5 4 3 2 1

Printed in China

Very special thanks to the people who helped make this book happen and who were inspirations for this book. To Keren Hazan and the entire Max Brenner marketing team, Dudu Vaknin, and the entire team from the Max Brenner Chocolate restaurants.
Special thanks to Uri Zohar and Danielle Sarna. To Yaniv Shtanger; Giora Bar-Dea; Alexey Kletzel; Yoram Aschheim, photography; Sarah Lagrotteria, recipe consultant; and Nachman Bensimon, chef consultant, thank you for all your hard work. And to Liron and Nellie, Efrat, Daniel, Eli, Hillel, and Mom and Dad.

Contents

Max

Almost always, when meeting someone for the first time, I'm asked how I actually started out making chocolate. I usually tell them that when I was ten years old, I read *Charlie and the Chocolate Factory,* by Roald Dahl, and I swore that, one day, I would find a river of chocolate and sail in it. I also tell them about Anna, who was my first love, and who could not fall asleep without eating a piece of milk chocolate before going to bed, because otherwise she would have bad dreams.

But the truth is that I wanted to be a writer. One that gets up at noon, sits in cafés, writes until the following morning and devotes a book to an impossible, eternal love.

At the age of twenty, I thought that in order to find inspiration for my first novel I needed to be alone. I needed to walk in narrow streets, sit in a dark room with a candle, feel the longing, and write. I went to live and work in the seventh arrondissement in Paris with a French chef who looked like Geppetto. I was an apprentice for six years. He taught me how to make toffee, marzipan, and nougat. He told me stories that are only passed on from teacher to pupil. I was lonely and did not write.

Later I started searching for romance as a source of inspiration. I wanted to live in a small house, ride my bicycle to work, make colorful sweets in big jars, and write. I opened a chocolate workshop. People fell in love with the movie that was my life. I was living the magic of romance, yet was making so many sweets that I had no time left to write.

Then I wanted to experience decadence to get a sense of real, raging inspiration—like the one described in the biographies of great writers. I wanted to wear Versace suits with tight pants, drink lots of wine, fall in love with the prettiest women, and write. I designed and created a lifestyle of chocolate with its own saying. I dived into decadence, but most of the time, I was drunk and did not write.

More than ten years have passed since I started looking for inspiration for my writing. I have yet to start writing. Recently, I bought a special feather pen and a thick leather-covered notebook. I am starting to write a novel soon.

I've been making chocolate for more than ten years. Almost without noticing it, I find myself telling its story. Maybe through the telling of its story, I can also tell something about myself, something about the longings, the romance—the decadence.

I invite you to watch, smell, taste, and feel my love story.

Yonatan

"Yonatan is not a man of words. You have to meet him in order to get to know him."

These are the words the friend who introduced us many years ago used, to tell me what I now know for myself—that Yonatan Factor is a man of drawings.

Today, however, as Yonatan and I are publishing an album of our work together, I want to switch places with him. For the first and perhaps only time, I wish to draw him in my own way, which is of course with words.

We planned to meet for the first time in South Tel Aviv, where Yonatan was born and still lives and is always just about to desert, to split from, because that's the way it is with stormy, sensuous love; like the kind he feels for the city that fills him with inspiration.

This is what he looked like at that first meeting: heavy brown hiking boots, a huge tattoo running up his leg that had been covered with a tattoo of a blue rectangle, because he was sick of what he'd loved the day before. Khaki shorts that reached his knees, a red kid's T-shirt. The body of the most muscular Irish boxer you can imagine, topped with a round head whose contours were hidden behind a pair of thick, black glasses that looked like they should be worn by a physics professor who never stopped reading. The spiky blond hair of a newborn chick. And even though you couldn't see it, stuffed inside was the romantic soul of a starving Russian poet.

He took me to eat at his favorite restaurant, a dive where the locals eat, and when I walked in I was convinced he'd actually taken me to see a play.

"This is what food should be like," he told me then. "Like a stage actor. Bathed in the bright light, in colors and sounds, with a strong text so it can express itself and bring out the magical personality hidden inside."

I didn't say a word. But late that night, when we left a dark bar together, I started talking and I've been talking ever since, and ever since then he's been drawing the most perfect scenery for our play that we've written together—our big chocolate stage play.

Chocolate

Chocolate is not just about taste. It is not just about mixing exotic spices or creating delicate mousses. It is absolutely not just an excellent gourmet product.

Chocolate, much more than other food, is associated with different aspects of life. It is a symbol of contradictory emotions and sensations.

On one hand, it is the most **romantic** gift; on the other, a **commodity** that is traded in the bourse.

It is sold like **precious** jewelry that is picked carefully from a crystal glass, but also is an **addictive** snack in every corner kiosk. It is tasted like a **fine** wine and licked straight from the bowl.

It is sexy. It is **nostalgic** and it's a **fantasy** object for children and grown-up children.

These diverse aspects of chocolate and of life are the inspiration for our book.

Dependable banana cupcakes

with dark chocolate chunks and a moody coconut sugar glaze

....

Just like every other morning, I entered the coffee shop across the street from my home. This morning you smiled at me. The cupcake was so fresh and the glass of hot milk more organic than ever. Now, just like every other morning, I understand anew that my taste changes according to your daily recipe of whims.

....

Banana Cupcakes
3 sticks unsalted butter

2 cups granulated sugar

6 large eggs

1 tablespoon vanilla extract

3 very ripe bananas, mashed

3 ¼ cups all-purpose flour

1 teaspoon baking powder

½ teaspoon baking soda

½ teaspoon salt

1 cup buttermilk

6 ounces dark chocolate chunks

Coconut Glaze
2 sticks unsalted butter, softened

1 tablespoon pineapple juice

1 tablespoon rum

3 cups confectioners' sugar, sifted

2 cups shredded coconut

1. Make the cupcakes. Preheat the oven to 350°F. Line two 12-cup muffin tins with cupcake liners.

2. In the bowl of a standing mixer fitted with a paddle attachment, cream the butter and granulated sugar until light and fluffy. Add the eggs one by one, then add the vanilla and mashed banana.

3. In a separate bowl, sift the flour, baking powder, baking soda, and salt together. With the mixer on low, alternate adding the dry ingredients and the buttermilk to the banana mixture, beginning and ending with the dry ingredients. Mix until just combined. Fold in the chocolate chunks.

4. Fill the prepared muffin cups two-thirds full. You should have enough batter to fill about half of a second tin. Bake until the tops are light golden brown and a skewer inserted in the centers comes out clean, about 25 minutes.

5. Make the glaze. Beat together the butter, pineapple juice, and rum in the standing mixer. Gradually beat in the confectioners' sugar until smooth. Spread over the cooled cupcakes and top with a cap of shredded coconut.

Yield: about 18 servings

Dependable Banana Cupcakes

with dark chocolate chunks and a moody coconut sugar glaze

Bohemian French toast chocolate sandwiches

made from classic honey butter brioche and painted with morning colors of crème fraîche and deep-berry red

I am sitting on the pavement outside the Café de la Paix in a pleasant tumult of people recounting to one another all sorts of important things. In the background, Dalida is singing a duet with Alain Delon about toffee and candies and chocolate and I imagine them walking in, taking a seat in the corner, drinking a glass of red, and whispering to each other all sorts of things so beautifully unimportant.

1 loaf day-old brioche (see page 28)
1 ½ cups milk
Zest of 1 orange
Juice of ½ orange
6 large eggs
¼ cup sugar
2 teaspoons unsweetened cocoa powder
½ teaspoon vanilla extract
½ teaspoon ground cinnamon
½ teaspoon salt
Unsalted butter, for cooking
2 bars dark chocolate, for shaving

Confectioners' sugar, maple syrup, crème fraîche, jam, sesame seeds, or other desired topping

1. Slice the brioche into ¾-inch-thick slices.
2. In a shallow bowl, combine the milk, orange zest, and juice. Whisk in the eggs until completely incorporated. Add the sugar, cocoa powder, vanilla, cinnamon, and salt.
3. Preheat a griddle or warm a large sauté pan over medium heat. Warm 1 tablespoon butter in the pan until it foams.
4. Lightly soak the bread slices in the egg mixture. Place several bread slices on the griddle and cook until golden brown, about 2 minutes per side. Repeat with remaining bread, adding butter to the pan as needed.
5. Shave a generous amount of dark chocolate onto each piece of bread and serve warm in stacks of three, letting the chocolate melt between the warm slices. Top as desired.

Yield: 4 servings

BOHEMIAN FRENCH TOAST CHOCOLATE SANDWICHES

MADE FROM CLASSIC HONEY BUTTER BRIOCHE
AND PAINTED WITH MORNING COLORS OF
CRÈME FRAÎCHE AND DEEP-BERRY RED

Dreamy warm Danish

with walnuts, creamy bananas, and chocolate cinnamon long-ago smoke

Only now, as the bulldozers raze the old confectionery, has the smell of cinnamon—no longer rising in the chimney—changed within our memory to the magical reality that we always wanted it to be.

Dough

3 large egg yolks, lightly beaten

3 ripe bananas, sliced

¾ cup milk, heated to 110°F

1 envelope dry yeast

4 ½ cups all-purpose flour, plus more if needed
   and for dusting

2 tablespoons granulated sugar

1 teaspoon salt

2 sticks unsalted butter

Filling

1 stick unsalted butter, softened, plus more for dotting

3 ounces dark chocolate, melted

1 cup packed brown sugar

¼ cup ground cinnamon, plus more for sprinkling

1 egg yolk, lightly beaten

2 cups walnuts, lightly crushed

1. Make the dough. In the bowl of a standing mixer fitted with a paddle attachment, beat the eggs and bananas on low speed until the bananas are lightly crushed, about 1 minute. In a separate bowl, stir the warm milk and yeast until the yeast dissolves. Pour the yeast mixture over the egg and banana mixture. Sift together the flour, granulated sugar, and salt. Cover the yeast mixture with about 1 cup of the flour mixture and let sit until the yeast rises and cracks through the flour cover, about 5 minutes. Turn the mixer to low and combine, gradually adding the remaining flour mixture.

2. Replace the paddle attachment with a dough hook and continue working the dough until it is sticky and smooth and pulls away from the side of the bowl, about 10 minutes. Add more flour if necessary to keep the consistency of the dough sticky. Turn out onto a lightly floured surface and work by hand for 5 minutes longer. Turn into a lightly greased bowl, cover with a clean kitchen towel, and chill in the refrigerator while you work the butter.

Chocolate: A Love Story, 16

3. On a lightly floured surface, pound the butter flat using a floured rolling pin. Fold the butter in half and pound flat again, pounding until the butter is workable. Using your hands, shape the butter into an 8-inch square.

4. Remove the dough from the refrigerator and place on a lightly floured surface. Roll the dough into a 16-inch square. Place the butter in the center of the dough square, then fold the dough over the butter from all four directions. Pinch the dough together at the seams to seal.

5. Lift the "package" and dust the counter again with the flour. Lay the dough down and use the rolling pin to roll the dough out to a large rectangle, about 12 by 16 inches.

6. Fold the dough in thirds by folding a short side of the rectangle towards the center. Then fold the other side over so it completely covers the dough, forming a square of three layers of dough. Place the dough back in the refrigerator to chill, about 30 minutes.

7. Remove the dough from the refrigerator and repeat steps 5 and 6. Do this one more time, resting the dough in the refrigerator for half an hour between each folding process.

8. Make the filling. Mix together the butter and melted chocolate. Stir in the brown sugar and cinnamon.

9. Return the dough to the lightly floured surface and roll out into a rectangle about ¼ inch thick. Whisk the egg yolk with 1 teaspoon water and lightly brush over the dough. Top with the chocolate filling and sprinkle with the crushed walnuts. Beginning with a long side, roll the dough up lengthwise.

10. Butter two 9-inch round glass baking dishes. With the seam side down, slice the dough log into ½-inch-thick pieces and place cut side down in the prepared dishes. There should be almost no space between the rolls. Brush the tops of the rolls with any leftover egg wash. Cover both baking dishes with plastic wrap and set aside to rise, about 40 minutes. Preheat the oven to 375°F.

11. Dot the tops of the rolls with butter and sprinkle with cinnamon. Bake until golden brown and puffy, 20 to 25 minutes. Serve warm.

Yield: 16 rolls

PATISSERIE

DREAMY
WARM
DANISH WITH WALNUTS,
CREAMY BANANAS,
AND CHOCOLATE
CINNAMON LONG-AGO
SMOKE

The American dream pancake

with Fifth Avenue milk chocolate maple syrup and red-berry SoHo salad

....

NYC, here I come. Uptown, Fifty-sixth Street and Madison. Expensive Armani suit and a platinum Rolex. Yellow cabs. Buckled up. Go downtown. Canal and Broadway. You want a suit? Just choose the tag: Dolce & Gabbana, Versace, Armani. A Rolex? Buy a pound. Up or down, who cares how? I'll be there.

....

Pancakes
1 cup milk
1 envelope dry yeast
½ cup all-purpose flour
½ teaspoon salt
2 large eggs, separated
Unsalted butter, for cooking

Topping
1 cup good-quality maple syrup
1 ½ ounces milk chocolate, chopped
1 teaspoon heavy cream
1 cup assorted fresh berries

1. Make the pancakes. Warm the milk over low heat until just warm to the touch. Pour into a large mixing bowl. Sprinkle the yeast over the milk and let dissolve, about 5 minutes.

2. Whisk the flour, salt, and egg yolks into the yeast mixture until the batter is smooth and lump-free. Cover with a clean kitchen towel and set aside to rise in a warm place, about 1 hour.

3. In the bowl of a standing mixer fitted with a whisk attachment, beat the egg whites into stiff glossy peaks. Gently fold the whites into the pancake batter.

4. Warm 1 tablespoon butter in a nonstick omelet pan or griddle over medium-high heat until it foams and subsides. Drop in the batter by 2-tablespoon-sized rounds and cook until the edges bubble and the pancakes turn golden brown, about 1 minute. Carefully flip the pancakes and continue cooking until golden brown but still soft in the center, about 45 seconds longer. Repeat with remaining batter, adding butter to the pan as necessary.

5. Make the topping. Bring the maple syrup to a simmer, then whisk in the chocolate and cream. Let cool slightly, then whisk until smooth.

6. Serve the pancakes hot with assorted berries and warm chocolate maple syrup.

Yield: 8 servings

The ameri can dream pan cake

with Fifth Avenue milk chocolate maple syrup and red-berry SoHo salad

The Belgian street waffle

with butterscotch chips, roasted pineapple and a white chocolate orange maple trap

···

Dough

3 ½ cups all-purpose flour
½ cup milk, plus more if needed
½ cup heavy cream
Scant ½ cup sugar
2 large eggs
1 envelope dry yeast
2 sticks unsalted butter, softened
1 teaspoon salt
2/3 cup butterscotch candies, chopped, plus more
    for topping

White Chocolate and Orange Maple Sauce

¾ cup heavy cream
8 ounces white chocolate, chopped
Zest of 1 orange
3 tablespoons orange juice
6 tablespoons maple syrup

Roasted Pineapple

1 stick plus 2 tablespoons unsalted butter
½ cup brown sugar
5 (½-inch-thick) pineapple slices

1. Make the dough. In the bowl of a standing mixer fitted with a dough hook, combine the flour, milk, cream, sugar, eggs and yeast. Mix on low to form a smooth dough, about 10 minutes. If dough is too dry or tough, add a little more milk 1 tablespoon at a time. Add the butter and salt and continue kneading until the dough becomes elastic and pulls away from the sides of the bowl, 10 to 15 minutes. It should not be sticky to the touch.

2. Let the dough rest in a lightly greased bowl at room temperature for about 1 hour. Turn the dough once and put in the fridge to rest for another hour. Turn it again and refrigerate for a minimum of 5 hours.

3. Add the butterscotch to the dough and mix well. Scoop the dough in heaping teaspoonfuls and roll into balls. Place the 10 balls on a baking sheet lined with parchment and let rise in a warm place for about 90 minutes.

4. Heat a waffle machine to 320°F. Add a ball of dough to each section on the iron. Bake until golden brown, about 3 minutes. Repeat with the remaining dough.

5. Prepare the sauce. Bring the cream to a simmer. Pour over the chocolate in a heatproof bowl and let sit until the chocolate begins to melt, about 1 minute. Add the orange zest and juice and stir until smooth. Let cool, then stir in the maple syrup.

6. Make the roasted pineapple. Melt the butter over high heat in a nonstick pan. Add the sugar and pineapple slices. Cook until golden brown, about 3 minutes per side.

7. Place a waffle on each of 10 plates, add half a slice of roasted pineapple, and top with white chocolate and orange maple sauce. Sprinkle butterscotch pieces over the tops and serve hot.

Yield: 10 waffles

THE BELGIAN STREET WAFFLE

with butterscotch chips, roasted pineapple and a white chocolate orange maple trap

Intimate Hungarian crêpes

with sweet white chocolate cheese, raisins, and dried fig hidden secrets

Shortly after it grows dark, I enter our secret place and sit in the corner, the spot that moves only us. Everyone comes to taste the famed crêpes of the Hungarian café that was once known only to us and is now full to capacity. I smile a tiny, pensive smile to myself: not one of these countless people will ever experience its true taste, the intimate taste created by you and me.

Filling

¼ cup dried figs, chopped
½ cup raisins, chopped
½ cup rum
1 cup cream cheese or farmer cheese
4 ounces milk chocolate chips
3 tablespoons honey
1 teaspoon ground cinnamon

Crêpes

3 large eggs
3 tablespoons granulated sugar
1 cup all-purpose flour
1 teaspoon salt
¾ cup milk
2 tablespoons brandy
3 tablespoons unsalted butter, plus more to grease
     the pan

Confectioners' sugar and ground cinnamon, for dusting

1. Make the filling. Soak the figs and raisins in the rum for at least 1 hour. Drain the fruit and discard the rum.
2. In the bowl of a standing mixer fitted with a paddle attachment, beat the cheese until soft and smooth. Mix in the figs and raisins and chocolate chips. Add the honey and cinnamon and keep beating until the mixture is combined and the cheese is soft and smooth, about 3 minutes. Set aside.

3. Make the crêpes. Whisk together the eggs and granulated sugar until they become a light lemony yellow. In a separate bowl, sift together the flour and salt. Whisk the dry ingredients into the egg mixture, whisking until smooth. Whisk in the milk and brandy. Cover and chill for at least 30 minutes before making the crêpes.
4. Preheat the oven to 200°F. Warm 1 tablespoon butter in a nonstick crêpe or omelet pan until it foams and subsides. Pour just enough batter into the pan to create a thin, even layer with a ladle or by rotating the pan. Pour any excess batter back into the bowl. When the bottom of the crêpe is slightly brown, flip and cook for a few more seconds.
5. Transfer the cooked crêpe to an ovenproof plate and cover with wax paper. Repeat with the remaining batter, adding butter to the pan when necessary and separating each cooked crêpe with a layer of wax paper. To keep crêpes warm while cooking the remainder, cover the top crêpe with aluminum foil and keep the stack in the warm oven. Crêpes are best eaten immediately but can be kept covered in the refrigerator for up to one day.
6. Spread the cheese mixture on the hot crêpes and roll as you would an omelet. Place on serving plates and dust the crêpes and plates with confectioners' sugar and cinnamon and serve immediately.

Yield: 6 to 8 servings

INTIMATE HUNGARIAN CRÊPES

INTIMATE
HUNGARIAN CRÊPES
WITH SWEET WHITE CHOCOLATE CHEESE
RAISINS AND DRIED FIG HIDDEN SECRETS

INTIMATE
HUNGARIAN CRÊPES
WITH SWEET WHITE CHOCOLATE CHEESE,
RAISINS AND DRIED FIG HIDDEN SECRETS

My one and only cocoa Crêpe Suzette

with mandarins, pistachios, and vodka

The breeze on the balcony touches his face gently. He is playing a slow tune on the violin. It's such a beautiful night. Through the tears that fill his eyes the flames are breaking into thousands of sparkling colors. Quietly he comforts himself and whispers: "You are not going to be mine, Rome, but you won't belong to anyone else."

Crêpes

3 large eggs
3 tablespoons granulated sugar
1 cup all-purpose flour
2 teaspoons unsweetened cocoa powder
1 teaspoon salt
¾ cup milk
3 tablespoons unsalted butter

Filling

5 tablespoons unsalted butter, softened
3 tablespoons superfine sugar
1 tablespoon vodka
Zest of 1 orange, preferably mandarin, plus more
    for sprinkling

Sauce

1 ½ cups orange juice, preferably mandarin
Confectioners' sugar, for dusting
½ cup vodka
3 tablespoons brandy

Chopped pistachios, for sprinkling

1. Make the crêpes. Whisk together the eggs and granulated sugar. Sift together the flour, cocoa powder, and salt. Whisk the dry ingredients into the egg mixture until the batter is smooth. Whisk in the milk. Cover and chill for at least 30 minutes.

2. Preheat the oven to 200°F. Warm 1 tablespoon butter in a nonstick crêpe or omelet pan over medium heat until it foams and subsides. Pour just enough batter into the pan to create a thin, even layer with a ladle or by rotating the pan. Pour any excess batter back into the bowl. When the bottom of the crêpe is lightly brown, flip and cook for a few more seconds. Transfer the cooked crêpe to an ovenproof plate and cover with wax paper.

3. Repeat with the remaining batter, and butter the pan when necessary, separating each cooked crêpe with wax paper. To keep crêpes warm while cooking the remainder, cover the top crêpe with aluminum foil and keep stacking in the 200°F oven. Crêpes are best eaten immediately but can be kept covered in the refrigerator for up to 1 day.

4. Make the filling. Combine the butter, superfine sugar, vodka, and zest, whisking until smooth. Place a crêpe, golden-brown side up, on a work surface. Spread 1 teaspoon filling in the center of the crêpe, then fold bottom up and over the center. Fold in sides of the crêpe to form a stuffed triangle. Repeat with the remaining crêpes.

5. Make the sauce. In a large pan, simmer the orange juice until reduced by one-third. Reduce the heat to low. Arrange the folded crêpes in a circle covering the bottom of the pan, overlapping if necessary. Baste with juice until they are warmed through, about 2 minutes. Place on serving platter and dust with confectioners' sugar.

6. Pour the vodka and brandy into a small saucepan and heat over a low flame. Do not allow to boil. With a long match, carefully light the alcohol and pour immediately over the crêpes. Sprinkle with orange zest and pistachios and serve.

Yield: 6 to 8 servings

my one and only
cocoa Crêpe Suzette
with mandarins, pistachios, and vodka

Veg-out chocolate cornflake TV wraps

with lazy Brazil nuts and coconut chocolate sofa dipping sauces

Wraps

5 crêpes (see page 24)
2 cups chocolate-hazelnut spread (recommended: Nutella)
5 bananas, thinly sliced
3 cups chopped Brazil nuts
3 cups sweetened cornflakes
2 cups shredded, lightly toasted coconut, plus more for garnish

Chocolate Sauce

²/₃ cup milk
8 ounces milk chocolate, chopped

Coconut Sauce

²/₃ (14-ounce) can coconut milk
1 tablespoon cornstarch, sifted
¹/₃ cup sugar
½ tablespoon coconut extract

1. Make the wraps. Place a room-temperature crêpe on a clean work surface. Spread a uniform layer of chocolate-hazelnut spread over the crêpe, sprinkle with some banana slices, chopped Brazil nuts, cornflakes, and coconut. Roll up. Repeat with remaining crêpes. Wrap each crêpe roll in wax paper and slice diagonally in two as you would a wrap sandwich.

2. Make the chocolate sauce. Bring the milk to a simmer and pour over the chocolate in a heatproof bowl. Let sit until the chocolate begins to melt, about 1 minute, then stir until smooth.

3. Make the coconut sauce. Place 3 tablespoons coconut milk in a bowl. Add the cornstarch and whisk until smooth. Place the remaining coconut milk in a saucepan and bring to a simmer. Whisk in the sugar. Add the cornstarch mixture, stirring until thickened. Remove from the heat. Stir in the coconut extract and let cool.

4. Place the sliced wraps on a tray and serve with dipping bowls filled with the chocolate and coconut sauces. Garnish the coconut sauce with a bit of coconut.

Yield: 5 wraps

VEG-OUT CHOCOLATE CORNFLAKE TV WRAPS

WITH LAZY BRAZIL NUTS
AND COCONUT CHOCOLATE
SOFA DIPPING SAUCES

VOL
+
−

1 2 3
4 5 6
7 8 9
0 X

TTX MIX

Control freak chocolate spread

with late-night toasted almond splinters on a crispy-munchy French brioche toast

Ladies and gentlemen, I would like to present the precise structure of the chronicle of lust: in the middle of the night, returning from a party and swearing a thousand times that it's just a touch, simply to feel, on the tip of the tongue, only once, and then giving in, full of longing, and disappointing yourself and deciding, without wavering or doubt, that now the technique for abstaining is absolutely clear—there will be no more next time, and I mean it for real.

Brioche

¼ cup warm milk

1 teaspoon honey

1 envelope dry yeast

1 ¼ cups all-purpose flour

1 teaspoon salt

2 tablespoons brown sugar

1 tablespoon hot water

1 ¾ sticks unsalted butter, softened

3 large eggs

3 ounces dark chocolate chips

Chocolate spread

2 sticks unsalted butter, softened

3 ounces dark chocolate, melted

3 tablespoons sweetened condensed milk

½ cup slivered almonds, toasted, plus more for sprinkling

Pinch salt

1. Make the brioche. In a small bowl, stir the warm milk and honey until the honey dissolves. Sprinkle the dry yeast over the mixture and stir again. Let sit until the mixture foams, about 5 minutes.

2. In the bowl of a standing mixer, sift together 1 cup flour and the salt. Make a well in the center of the bowl by pushing the flour toward the sides. Pour the yeast mixture into the center of the well. Sift the remaining ¼ cup flour over the yeast mixture to cover. Set aside in a warm place until the yeast rises and cracks through the flour cover, 10 to 15 minutes.

3. In a separate bowl, stir the brown sugar and hot water until the sugar dissolves. Add to the yeast in the center of the flour well. Using the paddle attachment on low, begin blending the yeast, flour, and sugar. Add the butter bit by bit and then 2 of the eggs, one by one. The mixture should begin to come together in dough form. Add the chocolate chips.

4. Replace the paddle attachment with a dough hook and work the dough at medium speed until smooth and sticky, about 10 minutes. On a lightly floured surface, continue kneading the dough by hand for about 5 minutes longer. Turn once in a lightly buttered bowl and cover with a clean kitchen towel. Set in a warm, draft-free place until the dough has doubled in size, about 1 hour.

5. After the dough has doubled, knead by hand for about 10 minutes. Shape the dough into a rectangle and place, seam side down, in an 8 ½ by 4 ½-inch loaf pan. Cover with a kitchen towel and let rise until doubled in size, about 1 hour.

6. Preheat the oven to 350°F. Mix the remaining egg with 1 teaspoon water and brush the egg wash over the top of the dough. Bake the brioche until the top is golden brown, 28 to 30 minutes. Remove from oven and let cool 15 minutes.

7. Make the spread. Combine the butter, chocolate, milk, almonds, and salt in the bowl of a food processor and pulse until smooth. Spread on piping-hot brioche. Can be stored in refrigerator for up to 1 week.

8. When the brioche has cooled, cut into ½-inch-thick slices and toast until golden brown. Top with the spread and sprinkle with almonds.

Yield: about 16 servings

CONTROL FREAK CHOCOLATE SPREAD

with late-night toasted almond splinters
on a crispy-munchy French brioche toast

Intimate scones

with tender milk chocolate chips and romantic winter's strawberry confiture

....

Through the window of our café, I watch as you heap butter and jam and fresh cream onto a golden pastry just the way we liked it. You serve it to his mouth and prove to me once again that romanticism is the mass market product of intimacy.

....

2 ¼ cups all-purpose flour

¼ cup granulated sugar

2 teaspoons baking powder

⅛ teaspoon salt

2 sticks cold unsalted butter, cut into small pieces

¼ cup finely chopped candied ginger

3 ounces milk chocolate chips

¼ cup heavy cream

1 large egg, lightly beaten, plus 1 for egg wash

1 teaspoon vanilla extract

Confectioners' sugar, for dusting

1. Preheat the oven to 375°F. Line a baking sheet with parchment paper or bakers' Silpat.

2. In a large bowl, sift together the flour, granulated sugar, baking powder, and salt. Using your fingers or two knives, cut in the cold butter pieces until you achieve a sandy texture. Stir in the candied ginger and chocolate. Add the cream, egg, and vanilla, mixing until just combined.

3. Place the dough on a cutting board and shape into a circle about ½ inch thick. Cut the dough into 8 triangles. Place the triangles on the prepared baking sheet.

4. Beat the remaining egg with 1 teaspoon water and brush the top of each scone with the egg wash. Bake the scones until golden brown, 15 to 20 minutes.

5. Remove the scones from the oven and set the oven to broil. Sift confectioners' sugar over the scones. Set the scones briefly under the broiler to brown, being careful not to let the sugar burn. Serve warm with clotted cream and strawberry jam.

Yield: 8 servings

INTIMATE SCONES

with tender milk chocolate
chips and romantic winter's
strawberry confiture

Plain Jane sweet chocolate rolls

with raisins, dates, and dried apricot influences

The house had been vacated. There was nothing left that they were not forced to sell; it was only on the table standing in the center of the empty, echoing space that they continued to serve the food on beautiful dishes. After all, one cannot forget that the essence of life does not change and will forever be determined by other people's taste.

1 tablespoon warm water
1 teaspoon honey
1 envelope dry yeast
4 ½ cups all-purpose flour, plus 1 to 2 cups for dusting
1 teaspoon salt
¼ cup roughly chopped dried apricots
¼ cup roughly chopped dates
¼ cup roughly chopped raisins
4 ounces dark chocolate chips
1 cup warm milk
1 stick unsalted butter, softened
¾ cup sugar, plus more for sprinkling
1 teaspoon vanilla extract
4 large eggs

1. In the bowl of a standing mixer fitted with a paddle attachment, combine the water and honey. Add the yeast and stir until the yeast and honey dissolve. Let the mixture sit until the yeast foams, 5 to 10 minutes.
2. Sift together the flour and salt. Stir in the apricots, dates, raisins, and chocolate chips. Set aside.
3. Mix on medium-low speed and gradually beat in the milk, butter, sugar, and vanilla. Continue mixing until thoroughly combined. With the mixer still running, add 3 eggs one by one. Slowly add the fruit mixture, making sure to stop when necessary to scrape any flour from the sides of the bowl. Continue mixing until the flour is completely incorporated.

4. Replace the paddle with the dough hook. Turn the mixer to medium and continue working the dough until it is smooth and sticky. Turn the dough out onto a lightly floured surface and continue to work by hand, about 5 minutes longer. Place the dough in a lightly greased bowl and cover with a clean kitchen towel. Set in a warm, draft-free place until doubled in size, about 1 ½ hours.
5. Line a large baking sheet with parchment paper or bakers' Silpat. Punch the dough down and cut into 12 equal pieces. Hold one piece of dough in both hands and, with your palms facing you, fold the edges of the dough away from you and toward the back of the dough, forming a small, tight ball. Roll gently to seal the ball. Place seam side down on the prepared baking sheet. Repeat with remaining dough pieces, making sure to space the balls 1 inch apart. Cover and let rise, about 1 ½ hours.
6. Preheat the oven to 375°F. Whisk the remaining egg with 1 teaspoon water and brush the tops of the buns with the egg wash. Sprinkle lightly with sugar. Bake until golden brown, about 15 minutes. Let cool before enjoying.

Yield: 12 rolls

Plain Jane sweet chocolate rolls

WITH RAISINS, DATES, AND DRIED APRICOT INFLUENCES

Plain Jane sweet
chocolate rolls
with raisins, dates, and dried
apricot influences

FOR SALE

Parisian new life chocolate dream cake

sprinkled in white powder sugar point of view

....

Dough (must be made 1 day ahead)

3 cups flour

⅓ cup milk

⅓ cup heavy cream

½ cup sugar

2 large eggs

3 tablespoons water

2 envelopes dry yeast

1 ½ sticks unsalted butter, softened

Pinch salt

Filling

½ cup heavy cream

4 ounces dark chocolate, chopped

1 ⅓ cups Nutella

7 ounces plum or strawberry jam

4 tablespoons unsalted butter

2 tablespoons cocoa powder

Confectioners' sugar, for dusting

1. Make the dough. In the bowl of a standing mixer fitted with a paddle attachment blend the flour, milk, cream, sugar, eggs, water, and yeast for 10 minutes. Add the butter and salt and continue mixing at a low speed until the ingredients come together and form a smooth elastic dough, about 10 to 15 minutes.

2. Place the dough in the refrigerator for 1 hour. Remove the dough and turn it once, then return it to the fridge for 2 hours more. Turn the dough again and return to the fridge for at least 12 hours.

3. Make the filling. Bring the cream to a boil and pour over the chocolate in a heatproof bowl. Let sit until the chocolate begins to melt (about 1 minute), then whisk until smooth. Whisk in the remaining ingredients until thoroughly combined.

4. Preheat the oven to 325°F. Divide the dough in half. Lightly dust a work surface with flour, then roll the dough into 8 by ⅕-inch-thick squares. Spread a generous layer of filling over each square. Beginning with the edge closest to you, roll the dough into 2 tight logs. Place the logs seam side down into 8-inch nonstick loaf pans. Bake until the cakes rise and a toothpick inserted in the center comes out almost clean, about 40 minutes. Decorate with confectioners' sugar.

Yield: 2 cakes (12 servings)

PARISIAN
NEW LIFE
CHOCOLATE
DREAM CAKE
SPRINKLED IN WHITE POWDER
SUGAR POINT OF VIEW

Modest carrot cake

with snobbish ginger confit, poetic medjool dates, and sophisticated wildflower honey

This week at an expensive restaurant I ate intricately composed dishes layered like poetry. Afterward, the meal and its philosophy were explained, and everyone sat wide-eyed in rapturous appreciation. I, too, applauded and set my face in an expression of intelligent fervor. Later, at home, I put on my pajamas, turned on the television, and watched a film about a soldier who parts from his beloved when she leaves forever for a faraway land. After that I poured myself a glass of hot milk and cut a slice of very plain cake baked without sophistication, which was so simply delicious it needed no philosophical explanation.

1 stick unsalted butter, softened
½ cup good-quality wildflower honey
2 large eggs
¾ cup milk
¼ cup orange juice
2 ½ cups all-purpose flour
2 teaspoons baking powder
½ teaspoon salt
3 cups freshly grated carrots (about 8 carrots)
½ cup chopped California dates
½ cup chopped candied ginger
6 ounces dark chocolate, coarsely chopped into chunks

Confectioners' sugar, for dusting

1. Preheat the oven to 350°F. Lightly grease a 9-inch round cake pan.

2. In a mixing bowl, beat the butter and honey until smooth. Add the eggs, one at a time, mixing well after each addition. Mix in the milk and orange juice.

3. In a separate bowl, sift together the flour, baking powder, and salt. Add the dry ingredients to the wet, mixing until just incorporated. Fold in the carrots, dates, ginger, and chocolate until just combined.

4. Pour the batter into the prepared pan and rap the pan a few times against the counter to knock out any air bubbles. Bake until the crust is a light golden brown and a skewer inserted into the center comes out clean, about 30 minutes. Cool on a rack. Dust with confectioners' sugar before serving.

Yield: 6 to 8 servings

MODEST CARROT CAKE

WITH SNOBBISH GINGER CONFIT,
POETIC MEDJOOL DATES, AND
SOPHISTICATED WILDFLOWER HONEY

Lipstick banana chocolate cake bonbons

enrobed in well-behaved white chocolate and a nutmeg lady's coat

Banana Cake

4 ripe bananas

1 stick unsalted butter, softened

1/3 cup sour cream or crème fraîche, room temperature

3/4 cup sugar

1 large egg, room temperature

3 tablespoons aged brown rum

1 1/2 cups all-purpose flour

1 teaspoon baking soda

1 teaspoon baking powder

1/4 teaspoon salt

3 ounces chocolate chips

Chocolate Glaze

1 envelope granulated gelatin

2 teaspoons cold water

1 cup heavy cream

Pinch ground nutmeg

15 ounces white chocolate, chopped

1 cup dried banana slices

1. Make the banana cake. Preheat the oven to 400°F. Butter and flour an 8-inch nonstick loaf pan.

2. In a bowl, squash the bananas with a fork and mix in the butter and cream until smooth. Gradually mix in the sugar, egg, and rum. In a separate bowl, sift together the flour, baking soda, baking powder, and salt. Add to the banana mixture, mixing until just smooth. Stir in the chocolate chips.

3. Pour the batter into the prepared pan. Place in the oven and reduce the heat to 325°F. Bake until puffy and golden brown, about 40 minutes. Let cool. Cut into 1-inch cubes.

4. Make the chocolate glaze. In a small bowl, combine the gelatin and water and let sit until the gelatin swells, about 3 minutes. In a small saucepan, bring the cream to a simmer, then whisk in the gelatin, stirring until dissolved. Add the nutmeg. Pour the hot cream over the white chocolate in a heatproof bowl. Let sit until the chocolate begins to melt, about 1 minute, then stir until smooth.

5. Dip the cake squares into the glaze and set aside to let the chocolate cool. Dip once again and then place a dried banana piece on top of each.

Yield: about 40 cake bonbons

LIPSTICK BANANA
CHOCOLATE CAKE
BONBONS

ENROBED IN WELL-BEHAVED WHITE
CHOCOLATE AND A NUTMEG
LADY'S COAT

Nostalgic dark chocolate cheese crumb cake

with a light blood orange inspiration

I am sitting in Herman Blum's café, where I have wooed each of my nostalgic loves. Without having to ask, I am served a piece of the legendary cheesecake, made only by Herman himself. I cut into it with the fork and let the beloved taste spread through my mouth, from the back of my tongue and to every part of my body. I close my eyes and remember. Although I have never met you I miss only you, my perfect love woven from a thousand memories of past loves.

Crumb Crust

1 stick unsalted butter, softened
1 cup sugar
1 ¼ cups all-purpose flour
6 ounces dark chocolate, chopped

Blood Orange Filling

1 envelope granulated gelatin
6 large egg yolks
1 cup sugar
1 pound cream cheese (*not* reduced-fat)
1 ½ cups heavy cream
Zest of 2 blood oranges
Juice of 1 blood orange
Juice of 1 orange

1. Preheat the oven to 375°F.

2. Make the crust. Using a hand mixer, cream together the butter and sugar until sandy in texture. Mix in the flour until you achieve a fine crumb. Press the crumb mixture into the bottom and up the sides of a 10-inch pie pan or a tart pan with a removable bottom to form a thick crumb crust.

3. Bake until golden brown, about 12 minutes. Remove from the oven and arrange the chocolate evenly over the bottom of the crust. Wait until the chocolate begins to melt, about 1 minute, then use an offset spatula to gently spread the chocolate evenly over the bottom of the crust. Set aside to cool completely.

4. Make the filling. Sprinkle the gelatin over a few tablespoons of cold water. Set aside to soften and swell.

5. Whisk the yolks and sugar together until thick and custardy. Add the cream cheese and beat until fluffy.

6. In a heavy-bottomed pan, bring the heavy cream, orange zest, and orange juices to a simmer. Whisk in the bloomed gelatin until dissolved. Remove from the heat and let the flavors infuse, about 5 minutes.

7. While beating the cheese mixture continuously, slowly drizzle in the warm, orange-scented cream. Do this slowly so as not to scramble the yolks. Whisk until completely combined. Set aside to cool.

8. Once the filling is cool to the touch, pour into the chocolate-lined shell. Cover and refrigerate overnight or for at least 6 hours before serving.

Yield: 8 to 10 servings

NOSTALGIC DARK CHOCOLATE CHEESE CRUMB CAKE

with a light blood orange inspiration

BLUME'S

Soft Decadence: Chocolate Cream Cake Creations, 41

Handsome tiramisu

of white chocolate, Irish Cream, and chic Italian espresso

....

Limoncello in a frozen glass. Paolo Conte is playing in the background while on the screen Sophia Loren and Marcello Mastroianni drive their white Porsche convertible into the distance along the winding lanes of Tuscany and into the screen that shrinks to a single point of focus, the sweet and true flavor of life: longing and dreams.

....

1 cup heavy cream
9 ounces white chocolate, chopped
1 ¾ cups strong coffee or espresso, cooled to room
    temperature
¼ cup Irish Cream liqueur
3 large eggs, separated
⅛ teaspoon salt
6 tablespoons sugar
1 ½ cups mascarpone cheese
18 large (4-inch-long) or about 40 small (2-inch-long)
    ladyfingers

Cocoa powder, for dusting

1. Bring ½ cup cream to a boil, then pour over the white chocolate in a heatproof bowl. Set aside until the chocolate begins to melt, about 1 minute, then stir the ganache until smooth. Set aside to cool.
2. Combine the coffee and Irish Cream in a shallow bowl. Set aside.
3. In the bowl of a standing mixer fitted with a whisk attachment, whisk the egg whites until frothy. Add the salt and continue mixing on medium until the eggs hold soft peaks. Gradually add 3 tablespoons sugar and continue beating until the whites are glossy and hold firm peaks.
4. In a separate large bowl, whisk together the yolks and remaining 3 tablespoons sugar until thick and pale yellow, about 3 minutes. In another bowl, stir the white chocolate ganache into the mascarpone. Gently fold the mascarpone mixture into the egg yolks until just combined.
5. In a clean bowl, whip the remaining ½ cup cream until it holds soft peaks. Gently fold the whipped cream into the mascarpone mixture. Finish by folding the egg whites into the mascarpone mixture until just combined.
6. Briefly dip the ladyfingers one by one into the coffee mixture. Use half the ladyfingers to line the bottom of an 8 by 8-inch glass dish. Spoon half the mascarpone mixture over the ladyfingers, then follow with a second layer of coffee-soaked fingers. Cover with the remaining mascarpone mixture. Cover and chill overnight. Dust with cocoa powder just before serving.

Yield: 6 to 8 servings

Chocolate: A Love Story, 42

handsome tiramisu

of white chocolate,
Irish Cream, and chic
Italian espresso

Soap opera chocolate cappuccino roulade

with polite toffee filling and white chocolate shavings

Grandpa and Grandma are sitting in the living room. Coffee with some whipped cream on top, served in porcelain mugs. A Wagner operetta is playing on the gramophone. A book by Schiller is open on the rolltop desk. Grandpa and Grandma are cultured. Quietly they pack Grandpa's suitcase. It is all very ordered, proper, as it should be. Exactly as it should be, after Grandpa's passionate love affair with the neighbor, which, properly, he does not discuss with Grandma, as it should be. Exactly as it should be between cultured people, exactly as it should be in human culture.

Sponge Cake
5 large eggs, separated
¾ cup granulated sugar
4 ½ ounces dark chocolate, melted and cooled
2 tablespoons espresso

Cream
¾ cup heavy cream
2 tablespoons espresso
3 ounces milk chocolate, chopped

Confectioners' sugar, for dusting
1 bar white chocolate, for shaving
1 cup toffee candy, chopped

1. Preheat the oven to 350°F. Butter and flour a 13 by 18-inch jelly-roll pan lined with parchment paper.
2. Make the cake. In a large bowl with a hand mixer, beat the egg yolks and ½ cup granulated sugar until the mixture is pale yellow and thick, about 5 minutes. Mix in the chocolate and espresso until just combined.
3. In a standing mixer fitted with a whisk attachment, whisk the egg whites until frothy. Gradually add the remaining ¼ cup granulated sugar. Whisk until the whites form glossy, stiff peaks.
4. Loosen the chocolate mixture with 2 large dollops of the egg whites, then gently fold in the remaining whites. Pour into the prepared baking pan, using a spatula to spread the batter evenly. Bake until puffy, but not dry, 10 to 12 minutes. Let cool completely.

5. Make the cream. Bring the heavy cream and espresso to a boil, then pour over the milk chocolate in a heatproof bowl. Let sit until the chocolate begins to melt, about 1 minute. Stir until smooth. Chill until cool. Beat the cooled cream with an electric mixer until it thickens into chocolate whipped cream, about 5 minutes.
6. Lay a piece of parchment paper on a level surface and dust with confectioners' sugar. Turn the sponge cake out onto the paper with a short side towards you, peeling away the parchment paper from the cake.
7. Spread the cake with the chocolate cream, leaving a ½-inch border all around. Sprinkle the cream with white chocolate shavings and toffee candy. Using the parchment paper under the cake to help you, gently roll the cake into a log.
8. Wrap the log in parchment paper and chill overnight. Remove the parchment and trim any rough edges from the roll. Dust with confectioners' sugar before serving.

Yield: 8 servings

Soap opera chocolate cappuccino roulade
with polite toffee filling and white chocolate shavings

Soft Decadence: Chocolate Cream Cake Creations, 45

Politically correct Sacher torte

with a loyal good taste

Shortly before winter, the Viennese papers were full of agitated news reports about the complete ban imposed by the government on the use of cocoa. Mention was made of the serious damage incurred by the famous Demel pastry shop, with Mr. Demel's picture alongside. But anyone who looked closely would discern a smile of joy on his lips, inexplicable in light of the circumstances, or perhaps perfectly explicable in light of the similar circumstances of the Sacher pastry shop, Demel's lifelong nemesis.

Cake

2 sticks unsalted butter, softened
¾ cup granulated sugar
8 large eggs, separated
½ teaspoon vanilla extract
6 ounces semisweet chocolate, melted
1 cup sifted all-purpose flour
1 teaspoon baking powder
½ teaspoon salt

Frosting

4 to 6 tablespoons boiling water or hot espresso
10 ½ ounces semisweet chocolate chips
1 tablespoon unsalted butter
1 to 1 ½ cups confectioners' sugar, sifted

Filling

1 cup apricot or raspberry jam

1. Preheat the oven to 350°F. Butter and flour a 9-inch round cake pan.
2. Make the cake. In a large bowl with a hand mixer, cream the butter and ½ cup granulated sugar until fluffy. Add the egg yolks one by one, then add the vanilla and melted chocolate. Mix until just combined.
3. In the bowl of a standing mixer fitted with a whisk attachment, whisk the egg whites until frothy. Add the remaining ¼ cup granulated sugar and beat until the whites form glossy stiff peaks.

4. Sift the flour, baking powder, and salt together, then mix into the chocolate mixture until just combined. Loosen the chocolate with a dollop of the egg whites, then gently fold in the remaining whites.
5. Pour the batter into the prepared pan. Bake until the cake has risen and a toothpick inserted into the center comes out almost clean, about 40 minutes. Let cool completely.
6. Make the frosting. Pour the hot water over the chocolate and butter in a large heatproof bowl. Let sit until the chocolate begins to melt, about 1 minute, then stir until smooth. Use a hand mixer to beat in the confectioners' sugar until the frosting is fluffy and smooth, 5 to 7 minutes.
7. Place the cake on a serving platter. Cut into 4 horizontal layers. Spread each layer with jam and reassemble the cake. Pour the slightly warm frosting over the cake, letting it drip down the sides. Set to chill in the refrigerator for at least 2 hours before serving.

Yield: 8 to 10 servings

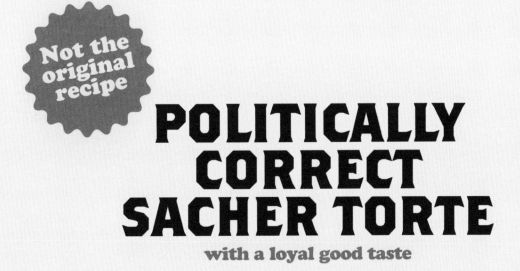

Macht nichts

Not the original recipe

POLITICALLY CORRECT SACHER TORTE

with a loyal good taste

Spy-thriller chocolate Black Forest cake

covered with Alpine whipped cream and cherry, the German double agent on top

....

10 large egg yolks

1 cup sugar

6 large egg whites

Scant ⅔ cup flour

⅓ cup cocoa powder

7 tablespoons unsalted butter, melted

2 cups heavy cream

⅓ cup confectioners' sugar

84 maraschino cherries

4 bars dark chocolate, for shaving

1. Preheat the oven to 350°F. Lightly grease a 12-cup muffin pan.

2. Whisk the yolks with ½ cup sugar until light yellow and custardy, about 5 minutes. In a separate bowl whisk the egg whites and remaining sugar until it forms soft peaks.

3. In a third bowl sift the flour and cocoa powder. Fold this mixture into the yolk mixture. Whisk in the melted butter and then gently fold in the egg whites.

4. Scoop or pour the cake batter into the prepared muffin tins, filling each tin three-quarters of the way full. Bake until a toothpick inserted in the middle comes out almost clean, about 25 minutes. Remove from the oven and let cool for about 30 minutes before turning the mini cakes out onto a cooling rack. Cut each cooled cake horizontally into thirds, keeping all the parts of each cake together.

5. With an electric mixer, whip the heavy cream and confectioners' sugar into firm peaks.

6. On a serving platter, place the bottom third of one mini cake, cut side up. Spread with a generous layer of whipped cream and place 3 cherries on top. Top with the next cake layer and spread with more cream, then add 3 more cherries. Place the top cake layer on top, spread an even layer of whipped cream on top and spread the cream all around the sides of the cake. Repeat with the remaining cake rounds. Freeze for 1 hour.

7. Using a vegetable peeler, shave the dark chocolate into a large shallow bowl. Carefully roll each cake in the chocolate peels. Decorate the tops of the cakes with a piped rosette of whipped cream and a last cherry.

Yield: 12 individual cakes

SPY-THRILLER CHOCOLATE BLACK FOREST CAKE

HELP

covered with Alpine whipped cream and cherry, the German double agent on top

My very own honey pie manifest

with roasted pecans, dark chocolate honesty, and beautiful vanilla essence

You hover in front of the kitchen window, colorful as a bright rainbow, touching and not touching the ravishing flower exploding before you, and you are so lovely . . . In spite of the poems I sent you and the conversations about the depth of the soul, you chose him. You know, if I were only as handsome as the two of you, I would make exactly the same choice as you, and, inflamed, I would become the chief prosecutor of my very own burnished theory of personality.

1 cup honey
3 large eggs, lightly beaten
3 tablespoons unsalted butter, softened
1 teaspoon vanilla extract
1 cup pecans, lightly toasted
3 ounces dark chocolate chips
½ teaspoon ground nutmeg
1 (9-inch) unbaked store-bought refrigerated pie crust

1. Preheat the oven to 325°F.
2. Bring the honey to a boil in a heavy-bottomed saucepan. Remove from the heat and let cool for about 2 minutes.
3. Whisk together the eggs, butter, and vanilla. Gradually whisk in the warm honey, followed by the pecans, chocolate, and nutmeg.
4. Unroll the pie crust and lay in a 9-inch pie plate. Pour the mixture into the pie shell. Bake until the top is golden brown and the center is set, about 25 minutes.

Yield: 8 servings

MY VERY OWN HONEY PIE MANIFEST

with roasted pecans, dark chocolate honesty, and beautiful vanilla essence

Cozy Option: Chocolate Pies, 51

Mon chéri chocolate cherry pie

with mascarpone dollops and mint-leaf youth memories

....

My dear, now that I am yours, I know that you will once again truly love me only in your memories. Mon chéri, maintenant que je t'appartiens, je sais que tu m'aimeras vraiment de nouveau seulement dans tes souvenirs.

....

2 (9-inch) store-bought refrigerated pie crusts
4 cups ripe cherries, pitted
1 ½ cups sugar
¼ cup tapioca
3 ounces dark chocolate chips
¼ teaspoon almond extract
1 tablespoon unsalted butter

Egg Wash
1 large egg yolk
1 teaspoon water

Mascarpone cheese, for serving
Finely chopped fresh mint leaves, for serving

1. Preheat the oven to 400°F. Unroll one of the pie crusts and use to line a 9-inch pie pan.
2. Mix together the cherries, sugar, tapioca, chocolate, and almond extract. Pour into the pie crust and dot with the butter. Unroll the second pie crust and lay over the filling. Crimp the edges of the two crusts together to seal the pie. Cut several decorative slits into the top crust to allow steam to escape.
3. Whisk the yolk and water together and lightly brush the top crust with the egg wash.
4. Bake the pie until golden brown and bubbly, about 45 minutes. Cool before slicing. Serve with dollops of mascarpone cheese and a scattering of fresh mint.

Yield: 8 to 10 servings

MON
CHÉRI CHOCOLATE
CHERRY
PIE WITH

mascarpone **DOLLOPS AND**
MINT-LEAF YOUTH MEMORIES

Cozy Option: Chocolate Pies, 53

Heaven-on-earth cocoa tarte tatin

made of golden apples with the red of the cheeks of a beautiful girl and caramel perfume

Eve, I am sure the garden is so beautiful, but if you want to live in harmony with your nature, I recommend life. Don't ever stop tempting me.

Dough

1 ½ cups all-purpose flour

2 tablespoons unsweetened cocoa powder

½ teaspoon salt

1 tablespoon granulated sugar

1 stick cold unsalted butter, cut into small cubes

1 large egg, lightly beaten

3 tablespoons ice water

Filling

¾ stick unsalted butter

1 cup granulated sugar

4 to 5 Golden Delicious apples, peeled, quartered, cored, and tossed with fresh lemon juice

Topping

½ cup heavy cream

1 teaspoon confectioners' sugar, sifted

½ teaspoon amaretto

½ cup thick Greek-style yogurt

Crushed walnuts, for sprinkling

1. Make the crust. Sift the flour, cocoa powder, and salt together. Mix in the granulated sugar. Add the cold butter cubes and, using your thumb and forefinger or two knives, "cut" the butter into the flour mixture until you achieve a sandy texture.

2. Make a well in the center of the flour mixture. Pour the egg into the well and incorporate the surrounding flour, adding ice water 1 tablespoon at a time until you achieve a smooth dough. Form the dough into a ball and flatten into a disk. Wrap tightly in plastic wrap and chill at least 2 hours and up to 1 day.

3. Preheat the oven to 400°F.

4. Make the filling. Melt the butter in a 12-inch oven-safe skillet over medium heat. Add the granulated sugar and let caramelize until golden brown. Add the apples in a single layer, cored side up, and cook until tender, 8 to 10 minutes.

5. Roll the dough into a 12-inch round about ¾ inch thick. Lay the dough over the softened apples, covering the fruit. Place the pan, apples, dough, and all, in the oven and bake until the pastry is golden brown, about 20 minutes. Lower the heat to 350°F and bake 15 minutes longer. Let cool about 5 minutes, then carefully invert over a serving platter.

6. Make the topping. Whip the cream, confectioners' sugar, and amaretto into firm peaks. Gently fold the whipped cream into the yogurt. Serve the tarte tatin immediately with generous dollops of the yogurt topping and sprinkles of crushed walnuts.

Yield: 8 to 10 servings

HeaveN-ON-eaRT H C OC Oa TaRT e TaT IN
made of golden apples with the red of the cheeks of a beautiful girl and caramel perfume

Cozy Option: Chocolate Pies, 55

A therapeutic chocolate pot pie

with a rich filling of soul-refreshing strawberries

Dough
3 ½ sticks unsalted butter
4 ½ cups flour
1 cup sugar
3 tablespoons cocoa powder
2 large eggs

Nut Crumble
7 tablespoons unsalted butter, softened
½ cup sugar
Heaping ¾ cup flour
1 cup hazelnuts, finely chopped

Cheese and White Chocolate Cream
Scant ½ cup heavy cream
8 ounces white chocolate, chopped
8 ounces cream cheese, softened
⅓ cup sugar
Seeds from 1 vanilla bean or 2 teaspoons vanilla extract
Zest of 1 lemon
1 ½ cups fresh strawberries, cleaned, hulled, and sliced in half

Egg Wash
1 large egg
1 teaspoon water

1. Prepare the dough. In the bowl of a standing mixer fitted with a paddle attachment, blend the butter and flour until crumbly. Add the sugar, cocoa powder, and eggs and continue blending until smooth. Separate the dough into 2 equal-sized balls. Wrap in plastic wrap and chill for at least 1 hour.

2. Preheat the oven to 325°F. On a lightly floured surface, roll one of the dough balls into a 15-inch-wide, ½-inch-thick round. Lay it over a lightly greased 12-inch pie plate and cover with a sheet of parchment paper. Weight the paper with dried beans or pie weights so that the dough will not rise. Bake for 15 minutes, then remove from the oven and let cool, about 30 minutes. Do not turn off the oven.

3. Prepare the nut crumble. Using a handheld mixer, cream together the butter and sugar until sandy in texture. Toss the flour with the hazelnuts, then add to the butter mixture, mixing until just combined. Cover and place in the refrigerator for 1 hour.

4. Line a baking sheet with parchment paper. Spread the crumble evenly over the baking sheet. Bake until golden brown, about 15 minutes. Remove from the oven and let cool, about 15 minutes. Keep the oven on.

5. Prepare the cream. Bring the heavy cream to a boil and pour over the chopped chocolate in a heatproof bowl. Let sit until the chocolate begins to melt, about 1 minute, then whisk until smooth. Add the cream cheese, sugar, vanilla, and lemon zest and stir until well combined.

6. Prepare the pie. Remove the parchment paper and beans from the baked crust. Sprinkle half of the nut crumble into the bottom of the pie, then spread the cream over the crumble, working from the center to the edges of the pie plate. Top with the strawberry halves and sprinkle with the remaining nut crumble.

7. Roll out the remaining dough ball until it is ½ inch thick. Gently lay it over the cream filling and strawberries and crimp the edges over the bottom crust to seal the pie. Cut a small decorative hole in the center of the crust to let out steam.

8. Whisk the egg and water together and lightly brush the top crust with the egg wash. Bake until the crust is golden brown, about 40 minutes. Serve warm.

Yield: 6 to 8 servings

A THERAPEUTIC CHOCOLATE POT PIE *with a*

RICH FILLING OF SOUL-REFRESHING STRAWBERRIES

Cozy Option: Chocolate Pies, 57

My lost childhood chocolate birthday cake

sprinkled with shiny colorful candy tears

··

When I was a little boy, I was always told there is no end to love. So perhaps that is why, each time I have a birthday, I am sad: On my birthdays I want love. I want all of it, and no matter how much I get I still think it's not enough. That somewhere out there in infinity, there are more of love's crumbs that were not handed to me. Today is my birthday. I lit some candles and made a lone plea: that next year, if at all possible, there'll be an end to love for me.

··

Cake

2 ½ cups all-purpose flour
2 teaspoons baking powder
½ teaspoon salt
1 ¾ sticks unsalted butter, softened
1 ½ cups sugar
4 large eggs
2 teaspoons vanilla extract
Sprinkles for decoration

Ganache

1 ¼ cups heavy cream
20 ounces dark chocolate, chopped

Syrup

1 cup water
1 cup sugar
1 tablespoon Cointreau

1. Preheat the oven to 350°F. Lightly flour and butter a 9-inch round cake pan.
2. Make the cake. In a small bowl, sift together the flour, baking powder, and salt. In a separate bowl, cream the butter and sugar with an electric beater until light and fluffy, about 3 minutes. Add the eggs one at a time, mixing well after each addition. Stir in the vanilla. Add the dry ingredients to the wet, mixing until just combined.
3. Pour the batter into the prepared pan. Bake until the crust is golden brown and a skewer inserted into the center of the cake comes out clean, 18 to 20 minutes. Set to cool on a cooling rack.
4. Make the ganache. Bring the cream to a simmer and pour over the chopped chocolate in a heatproof bowl. Let sit until the chocolate begins to melt, about 1 minute, then beat with an electric mixer until the ganache is fluffy and smooth. Let cool to room temperature.
5. Make the syrup. Bring the water and sugar to a boil in a heavy-bottomed saucepan. Lower the heat and simmer until the sugar dissolves, about 10 minutes. Stir in the Cointreau and remove from the heat.
6. Cut the cake horizontally into 2 layers. Brush the still-warm cake with the syrup (do not soak). Once the syrup is absorbed, spread the cooled ganache frosting generously over the top of one round. Top with the second layer of cake and cover with the remaining ganache, using an offset spatula to smooth the ganache down and around the sides of the cake.
7. Sprinkle liberally with multicolored sprinkles.

Yield: 8 to 10 servings

Chocolate: A Love Story, 58

MY LOST
CHILDHOOD
CHOCOLATE
BIRTHDAY
CAKE

SPRINKLED WITH SHINY COLORFUL CANDY TEARS

A philosophical highly concentrated fudge brownie

made of 70 percent dark chocolate thoughts

....

And then, from within the enormous emptiness, a dense sweetness begins, nearly burns, deep inside the throat, and from there to the eyes, since it is precisely when I am sad that the world seems to me more than ever so dejectedly optimistic.

....

2 sticks unsalted butter
1 cup heavy cream
32 ounces dark (preferably 70 percent) chocolate, roughly chopped
1 tablespoon vanilla extract
6 large eggs, room temperature
1 ½ cups sugar
1 cup all-purpose flour
1 teaspoon salt
1 ½ cups chopped walnuts

1. Preheat the oven to 350°F. Butter and flour a 13 by 18-inch jelly-roll pan lined with parchment paper.
2. In a large saucepan over medium heat, bring the butter and cream to a boil. Pour over the chocolate in a large heatproof bowl. Let sit until the chocolate begins to melt, about 1 minute, then stir until the chocolate has melted completely and the mixture is smooth. Set aside to cool.
3. Add the vanilla to the cooled chocolate mixture. Whisk in the eggs one by one, followed by the sugar.
4. Sift ¾ cup flour with the salt, and stir into the chocolate mixture using a wooden spoon. Mix until fully incorporated. Toss the walnuts with the remaining ¼ cup flour and mix into the batter.
5. Pour the batter into the prepared pan. Bake until a toothpick inserted in the middle comes out almost clean, 28 to 30 minutes. Let cool, then wrap and refrigerate overnight for the fudgiest texture.

Yield: 20 to 25 brownies

A PHILOSOPHICAL
HIGHLY CONCENTRATED
FUDGE BROWNIE
made of 70 percent dark chocolate thoughts

Such a beautiful chocolate soufflé

with an inner explosive warm chocolate personality

You sit here facing me, as attractive as ever, reciting from the last article you read about the importance of sharing inner feelings in relationships versus the superficiality of externalized beauty, and now, as I look at you, wrapped in your snugness, I understand with complete lucidity the deepest meaning of the term "inner beauty."

5 tablespoons unsalted butter

3 tablespoons all-purpose flour

1 cup milk

6 ounces dark chocolate (preferably 70 percent cocoa solids), chopped

4 large eggs, separated

2 tablespoons amaretto

⅛ teaspoon cream of tartar

¼ cup sugar

Lightly sweetened softly whipped cream, for serving

Note: You can butter the dishes, prepare the sauce (through step 2), chop the chocolate, and separate the eggs up to 4 hours ahead; cover sauce and eggs separately and chill. Stir sauce over low heat until hot before proceeding.

1. Preheat the oven to 375°F. Generously butter four 1 to 1 ¼-cup soufflé ramekins or one 1 ½-quart soufflé dish with 2 tablespoons butter. If using small ramekins, space them slightly apart on a large baking sheet.

2. In a large pan over medium heat, melt the remaining 3 tablespoons butter. Add the flour and stir until the mixture is smooth and bubbling. Add the milk, stirring continuously, until the sauce boils and thickens, about 2 minutes. Remove from heat. Add the chocolate and stir until smooth. Whisk in the egg yolks and amaretto and stir until blended and smooth. Set aside to cool.

3. In the bowl of a standing mixer fitted with a whisk attachment, beat the egg whites until foamy. Add the cream of tartar and keep beating on high. Gradually add the sugar and continue beating until the whites form glossy stiff peaks. Mix a third of the egg whites into the chocolate sauce to lighten, then gently fold that mixture back into the remaining egg whites until just combined. Gently pour the mixture into the prepared dish(es).

4. Bake until the soufflé(s) rise and the edges are set and dry but the insides are still creamy, 12 to 15 minutes for the small soufflés, or 15 to 20 minutes for the large one. For a fully set center, bake until the surface appears set and fairly dry, 2 to 3 minutes longer for the small soufflés, 5 to 6 minutes longer for the large one.

5. Serve at once, scooping portions from the single soufflé with a large spoon. Offer whipped cream to taste.

Yield: 4 to 6 servings

SUCH A
BEAUTIFUL
CHOCOLATE
SOUFFLE

WITH AN INNER EXPLOSIVE
WARM CHOCOLATE PERSONALITY

Happy Addiction: Concentrated Chocolate, 63

A high school bonfire chocolate melting heart cake

with a soft marshmallow first memory hidden inside

. . . .

Ganache Filling

½ cup heavy cream

7 ounces whole large marshmallows, plus 10 marshmallows, finely diced

7 ½ ounces white chocolate, roughly chopped

15 1 ½-inch by 1-inch deep silicon molds

Soufflés

12 ounces dark chocolate (preferably 56 percent cocoa), roughly chopped

3 sticks unsalted butter

1 ½ cups sugar

8 large eggs, room temperature

2 cups all-purpose flour

1 tablespoon unsweetened cocoa powder

1 teaspoon baking powder

15 soufflé ramekins, 2 to 2 ½ inches in diameter

1. Make the ganache filling. In a small saucepan, cook the cream and the whole marshmallows until the marshmallows melt and the mixture comes to a simmer. Pour over the white chocolate in a heatproof bowl. Let sit until the chocolate begins to soften, about 1 minute, then stir until smooth.

2. Divide the ganache among fifteen 1 ½-inch round by 1-inch deep silicon molds, sprinkling with the diced marshmallow as you go. Freeze for a minimum of 4 hours.

3. Prepare the soufflés. Preheat the oven to 400°F. Melt the dark chocolate in a heatproof bowl set over simmering water (a bain-marie). Add the butter and sugar and stir until the mixture is smooth and warm. Remove from the heat and let cool. Whisk in the eggs one by one. Set aside.

4. In a separate bowl, sift together the flour, cocoa powder, and baking powder. Whisk the dry ingredients into the chocolate mixture until smooth. Divide among fifteen 2 ½-inch paper baking cups, filling each three-fourths full.

5. Put one frozen marshmallow ganache piece in the middle of each baking cup. Bake until the soufflés rise and the insides are still molten, about 9 minutes. Serve immediately.

Yield: 15 servings

Chocolate: A Love Story, 64

a high school bonfire chocolate melting heart cake with a soft marsh mallow first memory hidden inside

Enticing sugar churros

dipped in spicy chocolate and chili pepper flamenco sauce

A curvaceous Spanish woman with creamy skin and flowing black hair reminds me each time to forget that lust is fleeting and love is eternal.

Churros

3 cups extra-virgin olive oil
1 cup water
10 tablespoons unsalted butter
1 ¼ cups all-purpose flour
4 large eggs, lightly beaten
Sugar for rolling

Chocolate Dipping Sauce

¼ cup heavy cream
1 tablespoon unsalted butter
1/8 teaspoon chili powder, or more to taste
1 cinnamon stick
4 ½ ounces milk chocolate, chopped

1. Make the churros. In a heavy-bottomed pot fitted with a candy thermometer, slowly bring the oil to 370°F.
2. While the oil warms, bring the water and butter to a boil in a medium saucepan. Boil 10 seconds before adding all of the flour at once. Use a wooden spoon to combine the water and flour into a sticky batter that pulls away from the sides of the pan. Stir until all the flour is incorporated into the batter. Remove from the heat.
3. Spoon the batter into the bowl of a standing mixer fitted with a paddle attachment. Beat on low until the batter cools, about 2 minutes. Gradually add the beaten eggs in three or four additions, mixing the dough until smooth after each addition and scraping down the sides and bottom of the bowl until all of the eggs are incorporated. You will know if you add too much egg at once if the batter curdles and it takes a while to

beat it back into shape—just keep beating until it no longer looks curdled. The dough should be of a pipable consistency and not too runny.
4. Cut wax paper into whatever shapes you want the churros to be—rounds, nests, straight strips, etc.—and oil lightly. Using a pastry bag with a large star nozzle, pipe the batter onto the wax paper shapes.
5. Using tongs, gently lift and place several churros, wax paper and all, into the oil with the churros face down. (Fry in batches so as not to crowd the pan and lower the oil temperature.) Use tongs to lightly dunk the churros for a few minutes, so that the hot oil seeps in between the batter and the wax paper. Continue frying the churros, turning or dipping occasionally to cook them evenly, until they are golden brown, 8 to 10 minutes in total.
6. Remove the churros from the oil and drain on paper towels. Repeat with the remaining batter. Pour sugar onto a tray. Roll the churros immediately in the sugar.
7. Make the sauce. In a medium saucepan, bring the cream, butter, chili powder, and cinnamon to a simmer. Remove from the heat and let the flavors infuse, about 5 minutes. Remove the cinnamon stick and bring the cream back to a simmer. Pour over the chocolate in a heatproof bowl. Let sit until the chocolate begins to melt, about 1 minute, then stir until smooth. Add more chili powder as desired. Serve warm for dipping with the churros.

Yield: 6 servings

ENTICING
SUGAR
CHURROS

DIPPED IN SPICY CHOCOLATE AND
CHILI PEPPER FLAMENCO SAUCE

Simple Luxury: Street Food and Gourmet Chocolate in Harmony, 67

Love and hate doughnuts

with dogmatic raspberry chocolate filling

Had one last night fresh from Elsa's son's bakery. They are getting so much better every year. Incredible! But will they ever top the memory of the immortal ones made by his mother, who passed away so long ago but never really agreed to leave?

Doughnuts

3 ½ cups all-purpose flour

1 teaspoon salt

½ cup granulated sugar

1 cup warm milk

2 envelopes dry yeast

2 large eggs, lightly beaten

3 tablespoons melted unsalted butter

Vegetable oil, for frying

Raspberry Chocolate Filling

¾ cup heavy cream

2 cups fresh raspberries

9 ounces milk chocolate, chopped

Confectioners' sugar, for dusting

1. Make the doughnuts. Mix the flour and salt in a large mixing bowl. Use your thumb to make a well in the center of the bowl, pushing the flour up the sides.

2. In a separate bowl, combine the granulated sugar and warm milk. Slowly pour the milk mixture into the center of the flour well (you want to keep the milk as separate as possible from the flour). Sprinkle the yeast over the top of the milk and, using a fork, lightly whisk the yeast into the milk, being sure to keep milk in the center of the well. Sprinkle a little flour over the milk. Set the bowl aside until the yeast foams and begins to puff up through the flour, about 20 minutes.

3. Using your fingers or a fork, begin bringing the flour into the center of the bowl, working the milk and flour into a dough. Add the eggs one at a time once the mixture becomes too dry. Add the melted butter and continue working by hand or with the paddle attachment in a standing mixer until you form a smooth dough. Continue working either by hand or with a dough hook for 5 to 8 minutes longer.

4. Turn the dough once in a lightly oiled bowl so all sides are oiled. Cover with a clean kitchen cloth and set aside until doubled in size, 1 to 2 hours.

5. Roll the dough until 3/8 inch thick and cut into 2 ½-inch rounds using a biscuit cutter or the top of a juice glass. Set the dough circles on a baking sheet and cover with a clean cloth. Set aside to rise again, about 30 minutes.

6. Fill a deep pot with enough oil to come halfway up the sides. Heat the oil to 365°F. Carefully slide several doughnuts into the hot oil, making sure not to crowd the pot. Fry until golden brown, about 1 minute per side. Remove with a slotted spoon to dry on a cooling rack. Repeat with the remaining doughnuts.

7. Make the filling. Bring the cream to a simmer. While the cream warms, crush the raspberries with the back of a wooden spoon or run briefly through a blender. Combine the raspberries and chocolate in a heatproof bowl. Pour the warm cream over the mixture and let sit until chocolate begins to melt, about 1 minute. Whisk until combined. You will still see raspberry seeds and have bits of delicious raspberry pulp.

8. When the doughnuts are cool enough to touch, use a pastry bag to pipe the raspberry filling through a hole in the bottom of each doughnut. Dust with confectioners' sugar and serve immediately.

Yield: 12 to 16 doughnuts

Guilt-free fried chocolate truffles

with generous extra cream of healthy happiness

1 ½ cups heavy cream
16 ounces dark chocolate, chopped
1 stick unsalted butter, softened
3 tablespoons almond or other liqueur
1 large egg, beaten
¾ cup all-purpose flour
1 cup shredded coconut
3 cups vegetable oil, for frying

1. Bring the cream to a simmer and pour over the chocolate in a heatproof bowl. Let sit until the chocolate begins to melt, about 1 minute, then stir until smooth. Beat in the butter and liqueur until thoroughly combined. Cover and chill for at least 2 hours.

2. Scoop the chocolate mixture with a mini ice-cream scoop or a teaspoon and roll into 1-inch (approximately 1 ounce) balls, powdering your hands with confectioners' sugar if necessary to keep the chocolate from sticking. Place on a baking sheet lined with parchment paper and freeze for at least 2 hours.

3. Prepare three shallow bowls: one with beaten egg, one with flour, and one with shredded coconut. Roll the frozen balls in each bowl: first in the egg, then in the flour, then in the egg again, and finally in the shredded coconut.

4. Let the balls rest for a few minutes in the refrigerator, then dip them again in all three bowls in the same order. Freeze the double-dipped balls for at least 1 hour.

5. In a deep pan, heat the vegetable oil to 375°F. Carefully fry the truffles, working in batches so as not to crowd the pan, until golden brown, about 2 minutes. Serve hot.

Yield: 30 truffles

Guilt-free fried chocolate truffles

with generous extra cream of healthy happiness

Painful white chocolate truffles

with crème de cassis rolled in sugar powder frustrations

Now he is standing, his arms crossed, in his unique shop—his dream's reality. He hopes with all his heart that the next customer to enter will also not purchase a thing, and will never understand his creation, and will provide him with a feeling of embittered arrogance, the sole and absolutely addictive pleasure that he is left with.

½ cup heavy cream
18 ounces plus 6 ounces good-quality white chocolate, chopped
2 tablespoons crème de cassis
½ cup confectioners' sugar, sifted

1. In a small saucepan, bring the cream to a simmer over medium heat. Pour the warm cream over 18 ounces of the chocolate in a heatproof bowl. Add the crème de cassis. Let sit until the chocolate begins to melt, about 1 minute, then stir until the ganache is smooth. Cover and chill for at least 6 hours or overnight.
2. Melt the remaining 6 ounces chocolate and set aside to cool. Sift the confectioners' sugar into a shallow bowl.
3. Depending on the size truffles you desire, use a teaspoon or tablespoon to scoop a portion of the chilled ganache. Using clean hands, quickly roll the scoop into a ball and drop gently into the cooled melted chocolate. Lay on a sheet tray lined with wax paper.
4. Repeat with the remaining ganache. If the ganache becomes too warm to work with at any point, place the bowl back in the refrigerator to chill for about 30 minutes. Chill the dipped truffles until the chocolate coating has set, about 20 minutes. Roll the truffles in confectioners' sugar until lightly coated. Chill the finished truffles for at least 2 hours before serving.

Yield: about 30 small or 18 large truffles

Chocolate: *A Love Story, 72*

PAINFUL WHITE CHOCOLATE TRUFFLES

with crème de cassis rolled in sugar powder frustrations

Max and Moritz profiteroles

with chocolate pastry cream spiced with mischievous coconut milk

The scent of warm dough mixed with brown caramel. Metal trays overflowing with golden pastries on the wire shelving at the window are winking to you to come in. The bakery is eternal, the baker is ageless. But Max and Moritz are at the counter standing in the queue like everybody else and buying their favorite childhood sweet, exactly like we always wanted them to be.

Filling (make 1 day ahead)
1 (14-ounce) can coconut milk (*not* light coconut milk)
1 ¼ cups milk
4 large egg yolks
¼ cup granulated sugar
⅓ cup cornstarch, sifted
3 ounces dark chocolate, chopped

Profiteroles
1 cup milk
1 stick unsalted butter
1 cup all-purpose flour
½ teaspoon salt
5 large eggs, lightly beaten

Topping
¼ cup heavy cream
1 teaspoon banana liqueur
4 ½ ounces dark chocolate

Confectioners' sugar, for dusting

1. Make the filling. In a heavy-bottomed saucepan, bring the coconut milk and milk to a boil. In a separate bowl, whisk together the egg yolks, granulated sugar, and cornstarch until thick and smooth. Temper the yolk mixture with a little hot milk mixture, then gradually whisk the remaining milk into the yolks, whisking continuously until smooth and thick. Pour back into the pot and whisk over low heat until the custard begins to thicken. Remove from the heat, mix in the chocolate, and let cool. Chill overnight.

2. Make the profiteroles. In a heavy-bottomed saucepan, bring the milk and butter to a boil. Sift the flour and salt together and add to the milk mixture all at once. Mix well with a wooden spoon until the flour is completely incorporated. Remove from the heat.

3. Spoon the batter into the bowl of a standing mixer fitted with a paddle attachment. Beat on low until cool, about 2 minutes.

4. Gradually add the beaten eggs in three or four additions, mixing until smooth after each addition. Scrape down the sides and bottom of the bowl until all of the eggs are incorporated. If you add too much egg at once it will be more difficult and take longer to combine. It will also look like it has curdled, but continued beating will bring it back.

5. Preheat the oven to 425°F. Line 2 baking sheets with parchment paper or bakers' Silpat.

6. Spoon the batter into a pastry bag fitted with a 1-inch round tip. Pipe onto the prepared sheets in 1 ½-inch mounds. Wet your fingertip and lightly press down upon the tip of each mound so that the top is smooth. Bake until golden brown and puffy, about 18 minutes. Turn the oven off and let the profiteroles sit inside for 10 minutes longer. Remove and let cool to room temperature.

7. Make the topping. Bring the cream to a simmer and whisk in the liqueur and the chocolate in a heatproof bowl. Stir until smooth.

8. To serve, cut the profiteroles in half horizontally and fill with the cream. Dip the very top of the profiterole "hat" in the chocolate topping. Reassemble the profiteroles, dust with confectioners' sugar, and serve immediately.

Yield: 25 profiteroles

Chocolate: A Love Story, 74

MAX AND MORITZ PROFITE ROLES

with chocolate pastry cream
spiced with mischievous coconut milk

Forever young white chocolate custard

perfumed with lemongrass and mixed with falling-in-love sweet wine lychees

Night. Candles. Lots of warm yellow candles reflecting and shimmering in a shiny sauce poured over sweet desserts. Colorful alcohol served with incandescent straws, as on a tropical island. It is crowded. Everyone is handsome as movie stars in the dim light that flickers over their faces, hiding a magical intimacy behind twinkling eyes. A voluptuous smell whispers secrets that intoxicate the people. Peter Pan flies about among the guests. Adults revert to being children. The grand soiree of sweets releases inside us, as always, the most beautiful feelings.

1 (20-ounce) can lychees, drained and chopped

½ cup sweet dessert wine (e.g., Muscat)

1 ¼ cups milk

½ cup sugar

1 stem lemongrass, lightly crushed

1 teaspoon vanilla extract

3 ounces white chocolate, chopped, plus 1 bar for shaving

1 tablespoon cornstarch

2 large eggs

1. Soak the lychees in the wine for 1 hour. Drain the fruit, reserving 1 tablespoon of the wine for the custard.

2. In a heavy-bottomed saucepan, bring the reserved wine and the milk to a boil. Add ¼ cup sugar, the lemongrass, and vanilla. Remove from the heat, cover, and let the flavors infuse for 10 minutes.

3. Remove the lemongrass from the milk mixture and discard. Bring the milk back to a simmer and whisk in the chopped white chocolate until the mixture is smooth. Remove from the heat.

4. Sift the cornstarch into a bowl. Add the eggs and remaining ¼ cup sugar and whisk until the mixture is lump-free.

5. Whisking the eggs constantly, slowly drizzle the warm milk mixture into the eggs. Keep adding slowly, whisking continuously until all the milk has been added. Pour the mixture back into the pot and then whisk over a low flame until the cream thickens to an almost pudding-like consistency, about 5 minutes. Do not overcook, as the pudding will thicken as it chills. Let cool at room temperature.

6. Gently fold the lychees into the cooled custard. Pour into individual serving bowls and cover with plastic wrap. Chill in the refrigerator for several hours or overnight. Top with white chocolate shavings before serving.

Yield: 6 servings

Forever young

WHITE CHOCOLATE CUSTARD

perfumed with lemongrass and mixed with falling-in-love sweet wine lychees

Alternative milk chocolate mousse

scented with comforting raspberry and white chocolate hugs

Chocolate is the substitute for love and will always be there for you.

¾ cup heavy cream
3 tablespoons unsalted butter
7 ounces milk chocolate, chopped
½ pint fresh raspberries, plus more for topping
2 large eggs, separated, plus 3 large egg whites
3 tablespoons sugar
1 tablespoon unsweetened cocoa powder, sifted
1 teaspoon salt

1 bar white chocolate, for shaving

1. In a small saucepan, bring the cream and butter to a simmer. Pour the hot mixture over the milk chocolate in a heatproof bowl. Let sit for about 1 minute, until chocolate begins to melt, then stir to form a smooth chocolate cream.
2. Puree the raspberries in a blender or food processor. Strain through a fine sieve; discard raspberry pulp. Whisk the puree into the chocolate mixture. Set aside to cool for at least 15 minutes.
3. When the chocolate raspberry cream has cooled, whisk in the egg yolks, one at a time. Set aside.
4. In the bowl of a standing mixer fitted with a whisk attachment, whisk the 5 egg whites until frothy. Gradually add the sugar, cocoa powder, and salt, continuing to mix until the whites form stiff glossy peaks.
5. Stir 2 large dollops of the egg whites into the chocolate raspberry cream to loosen it up, then gently fold in the remaining whites. Cover the mousse with plastic wrap and chill at least 6 hours or overnight. Serve chilled with shavings of white chocolate and fresh raspberries.

Yield: 8 to 10 servings

ALTERNATIVE MILK CHOCOLATE MOUSSE

*scented with comforting raspberry
and white chocolate hugs*

A mannered white chocolate crème brûlée

with jasmine and fresh cherries in sweet kirsch d'Alsace

My Maud, I want you to know: it's your French accent when you speak English that makes any food divine and not the fresh ingredients you bought in the market, as you explain to me the importance of their finesse.

12 firm ripe cherries, pitted and halved

¼ cup kirsch

1 ¼ cups heavy cream

2 bags (approximately 1.3 ounces each) jasmine tea leaves

1 teaspoon vanilla extract

7 large egg yolks, plus 1 large egg

½ cup sugar, plus more for topping

1 ½ ounces white chocolate chips

1. Soak the cherries in the kirsch at least 1 hour. Drain, discard the kirsch, and divide the cherry halves among 6 lightly buttered ramekins. Set the ramekins aside in a large baking dish.

2. Preheat the oven to 325°F.

3. In a small saucepan, bring the cream to a simmer. Add the tea bags and vanilla and remove from the heat. Let the cream steep for 20 to 30 minutes.

4. In a large heatproof mixing bowl set over simmering water (a bain-marie), whisk the egg yolks, egg, and the sugar until pale yellow and thick, about 3 minutes. Remove from the heat.

5. Discard the tea bags and bring the cream back to a simmer. Whisk in the white chocolate. Gradually drizzle the warm cream into the egg mixture, whisking continuously so the eggs do not cook. Divide evenly among the 6 ramekins.

6. Pour the hot water from the bain-marie into the baking dish so that the water comes halfway up the sides of the ramekins. Bake until set and lightly golden, about 30 minutes. Let cool and then chill overnight.

7. Preheat the broiler. Sprinkle the top of each crème brûlée with a thin layer of sugar and place under the broiler until the sugar is golden brown and bubbly. Serve immediately.

Yield: 6 servings

A MANNERED WHITE CHOCOLATE CRÈME BRÛLÉE

WITH JASMINE AND FRESH CHERRIES IN SWEET KIRSCH D'ALSACE

Eco-friendly chocolate bread pudding

made of all the leftovers and so good that none is left over

1 ½ cups whole milk
2 cups heavy cream
9 ounces dark chocolate, chopped, plus 3 ounces
3 large eggs, plus 3 large egg yolks
½ cup sugar
12 brioche buns or 1 loaf white bread, cubed

1. Preheat the oven to 325°F. Bring the milk and cream to a boil and pour over three-quarters of the chocolate in a heatproof bowl. Cover and let sit until the chocolate begins to melt, about 1 minute. Stir until smooth.
2. In a separate bowl, whisk the eggs, egg yolks, and sugar until well combined. Keep mixing and stir in the chocolate mixture.
3. Place the brioche cubes in a large bowl. Pour the chocolate custard mixture over the brioche. Add the remaining chopped chocolate and stir well to combine. Set aside to let the custard soak into the bread, about 10 minutes, then pour into two 8-inch loaf pans. Bake until golden brown and crusty and a toothpick inserted into the center comes out clean, about 30 minutes.
4. Remove from the oven and let cool 20 minutes before unmolding. Cut into 1-inch slices and serve with the vanilla cream.

Vanilla Cream
2 tablespoons cornstarch
2 ½ cups milk, divided
½ cup sugar
2 large egg yolks
1 vanilla bean, split lengthwise, or 1 teaspoon
   vanilla extract

1. Sprinkle the cornstarch over ½ cup of the milk in a small bowl and whisk to dissolve. Add the sugar and egg yolks and whisk well.
2. Bring the remaining 2 cups milk and the vanilla bean just to a simmer in a heavy-bottomed medium saucepan over low heat. (If using vanilla extract, add it in step 3.) Remove the bean, scrape the vanilla seeds into the milk, and discard the bean. Gradually whisk the egg yolk mixture into the milk.
3. Cook, whisking often, until the sauce comes to a full boil, about 3 minutes. If using vanilla extract, stir it in now. Strain through a wire sieve into a bowl. Serve warm.

Yield: 16 servings

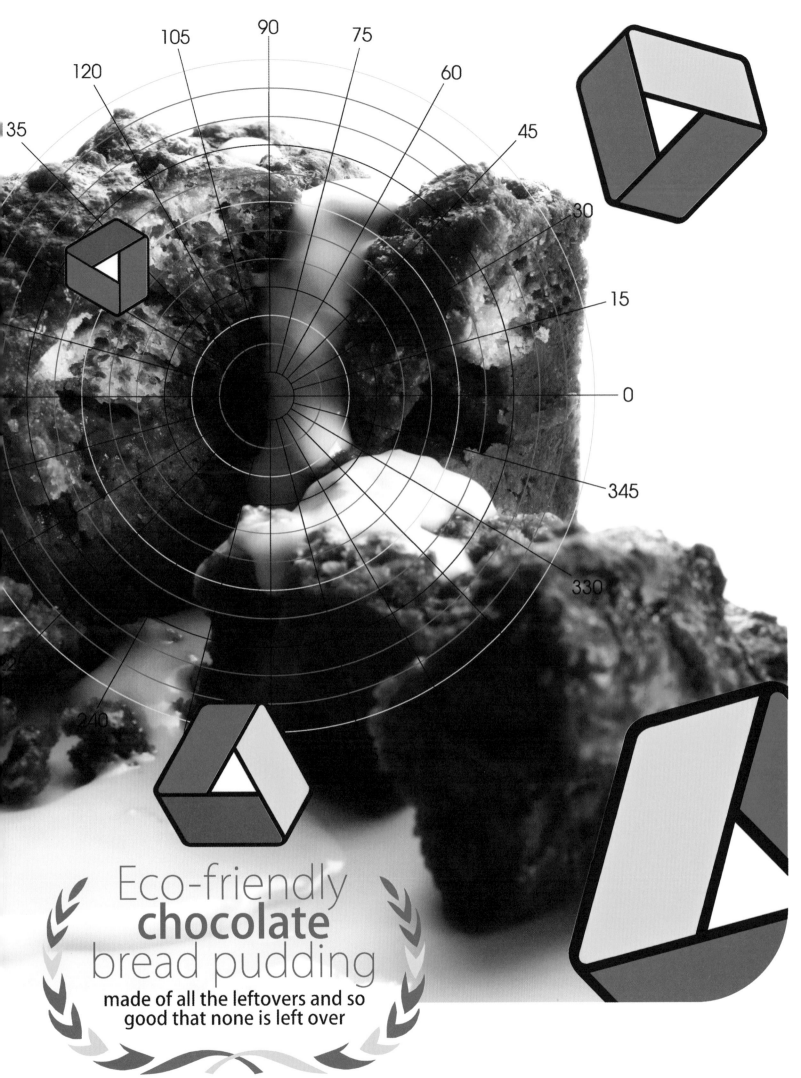

Eco-friendly **chocolate** bread pudding

made of all the leftovers and so good that none is left over

Revolutionary rice pudding

with dates, capitalistic dried cranberries, and forbidden dark chocolate brandy sauce

Can I get exactly the rice pudding that I like? No big dramas, no heroic revolutions. Changes in life's basics are totally unacceptable . . .

Rice Pudding

5 cups whole milk

1 ½ cups jasmine rice

Pinch salt

1 cup heavy cream

½ cup brandy

¾ cup sugar

½ cup dates, finely chopped

½ cup dried apricots, finely chopped

½ cup dried cranberries, finely chopped

6 large egg yolks

3 tablespoons unsalted butter, for preparing the ramekins

Chocolate Brandy Sauce

½ cup heavy cream

1 tablespoon unsalted butter

9 ounces dark chocolate, chopped

1 tablespoon brandy

1. Make the rice. In a medium-sized saucepan, bring 4 cups milk to a boil, then lower to a simmer. Whisk in the rice and salt. Cover and simmer until the rice is tender, about 40 minutes.

2. Preheat the oven to 325°F. Bring 4 cups water to a boil.

3. Mix the remaining 1 cup milk, the cream, brandy, sugar, dates, apricots, and cranberries into the rice.

4. Temper the yolks by adding a few spoonfuls of the warm rice mixture to the yolks, mixing to combine. Add the warm yolks to the rice mixture, stirring until well combined.

5. Lightly grease 6 to 8 soufflé ramekins with the butter and place inside a large baking dish. Fill the ramekins with the pudding mixture, making sure to stir well between each addition. Pour the boiling water into the baking dish so it comes halfway up the sides of the ramekins. Bake until the puddings are set around the edges but still soft in the middle, about 25 minutes. Remove the puddings from the baking dish and let sit at room temperature for about 10 minutes.

6. Meanwhile, make the sauce. Bring the cream and butter to a boil. Pour over the dark chocolate and brandy in a heatproof bowl. Let sit until the chocolate begins to melt (about 1 minute), then whisk until smooth. Keep warm.

7. Serve the puddings warm with puddles of the warm chocolate brandy sauce.

Yield: 6 to 8 servings

REVOLUTIONARY RICE PUDDING

WITH DATES,
CAPITALISTIC DRIED
CRANBERRIES, AND FORBIDDEN
**DARK CHOCOLATE
BRANDY SAUCE**

Military porridge

with toffee and a big chunk of chocolate heartbreak melting in the middle

· ·

My love, three years have passed since I last saw you. So many things are changing around me and the war seems endless. Only this late afternoon ritual, standing in the long line of soldiers in front of the huge aluminum saucepans covered with steam leaves me with the feeling that after all there are some things that never change in life. Still waiting for your letter.

· ·

Porridge

2 ½ cups milk, plus more if desired

1 teaspoon salt

¾ cup semolina flour

Toffee

1 ½ cups sugar

3 tablespoons water

¼ cup heavy cream

4 1-ounce milk chocolate chunks, for topping

1. Make the porridge. In a medium saucepan, bring the milk to a simmer. Slowly whisk in the salt and flour, swapping the whisk for a wooden spoon once the porridge thickens. Add more milk if desired for a thinner consistency. Keep warm.

2. Make the toffee. Combine the sugar and water in a small saucepan over medium-high heat. Cook, swirling occasionally, until a golden-brown caramel forms, about 8 minutes. Standing away from the pot so as to avoid any splatters, slowly add the cream to stop the caramel from turning darker. Stir to form a rich, smooth caramel. Cook for another minute, then remove from the heat and let cool for 2 to 3 minutes.

3. Portion the warm porridge into 4 breakfast bowls and carefully spoon some of the hot caramel on top of each serving. Place a big chunk of milk chocolate in the center of each bowl. Let the chocolate melt inside.

Yield: 4 servings

MILITARY PORRIDGE

WITH TOFFEE AND A BIG CHUNK OF CHOCOLATE HEARTBREAK MELTING IN THE MIDDLE

Pretentious white chocolate panna cotta

with chi-chi pears in grenadine

After searching extensively, this week I acquired a pet chef for myself, the kind that no one else has. He is mine and only mine, unknown, and he prepares delicate creams with rare spices and rare chocolate mixed with rare champagne. Now, with this new find secreted away in my possession, I can at long last proclaim and define myself clearly: there is no one else like me on the face of the earth, I love me so dearly!

Panna Cotta

1 envelope granulated gelatin

3 tablespoons water

1 ¾ cups milk

1 ¾ cups heavy cream

Scant ½ cup sugar

3 ounces white chocolate, coarsely chopped

1 teaspoon vanilla extract

Pears

4 cups water

2 cups sugar

3 tablespoons grenadine

3 small firm pears, peeled, cored, and halved lengthwise

1. Lightly butter 6 individual ramekins.

2. Make the panna cotta. In a small bowl, sprinkle the gelatin over the water until it softens and swells. Heat the milk and cream in a saucepan, but do not boil. Remove from the heat. Whisk the gelatin and sugar into the milk until dissolved. Pour the milk mixture over the white chocolate and vanilla in a heatproof bowl. Let sit until the chocolate begins to melt, about 1 minute, then whisk to combine. Divide the mixture equally among the prepared ramekins. Cover and chill overnight.

3. Prepare the pears. In a heavy-bottomed pot, bring the water and sugar to a boil. Reduce the heat and simmer until the sugar dissolves, about 5 minutes. Stir in the grenadine. Add the pears and enough water to keep the pears submerged in the syrup. Simmer until the pears are knife-tender, about 12 minutes. Remove the pears from the poaching liquid, cover, and chill overnight. Continue simmering the poaching liquid until it is reduced to a thin syrup. Chill syrup overnight.

4. To serve, run a kitchen towel under hot water and fold in half on a work surface. Place the ramekins on top to help loosen the custard. With a sharp knife, loosen the custard from the sides of the dishes and invert each ramekin onto a dessert plate. Spoon a little grenadine syrup over each custard and top with poached pear slices.

Yield: 6 servings

PRETENTIOUS WHITE CHOCOLATE PANNA COTTA

WITH CHI-CHI PEARS IN GRENADINE

Kinky Pavlova

with contradicting characteristics of emotional red berries and late-night sexy dark chocolate cream

Always, at the end, you would feed me strawberries and cream. That was your fetish. Truth is, we had nothing in common but outstanding lovemaking and lots of the most tender feelings and mutual understanding, and love, so much love. We never talked about anything. Truth is, we had nothing in common but outstanding lovemaking.

Pavlova

4 large egg whites
1 teaspoon white vinegar
1 cup superfine sugar
1 teaspoon cornstarch, sifted
½ teaspoon vanilla extract

Dark Chocolate Cream

2 cups heavy cream
½ teaspoon vanilla extract
3 ounces dark chocolate, chopped
About 2 teaspoons confectioners' sugar

½ pint fresh raspberries
½ pint fresh blueberries
1 cup sliced strawberries

1. Preheat the oven to 250°F. Line a large baking sheet with parchment paper or bakers' Silpat.

2. Make the pavlova. In the bowl of a standing mixer with a whisk attachment, whisk the egg whites and vinegar at high speed until soft peaks form.

3. Gradually add the superfine sugar 1 tablespoon at a time, mixing well after each addition. Once all the sugar has been mixed in, add the cornstarch and vanilla. Mix until blended and forming stiff, shiny peaks that feel smooth between your fingers.

4. Spoon the meringue into a large mound in the center of the prepared sheet, forming two 7- to 8-inch circles, or one large circle.

5. Bake for 1 hour, then reduce the oven to 200°F and bake for 1 hour longer, or until the outside is dry and slightly crispy. The inside should still be soft. Turn off the oven, open the door a little and allow the meringue to cool completely.

6. Make the chocolate cream. Bring the cream and vanilla to a boil and pour over the chocolate in a heatproof bowl. Let sit until the chocolate begins to melt, about 1 minute, then stir until smooth. Chill until cold to the touch, at least 1 hour. Using a hand mixer or chilled whisk, whip the chocolate cream into soft mounds of whipped cream, adding the confectioners' sugar as desired.

7. Transfer the cooled meringue to a serving plate. Top with generous dollops of the chocolate whipped cream. Add fruit as desired and serve immediately.

Yield: 6 to 8 servings

Chocolate: A Love Story, 90

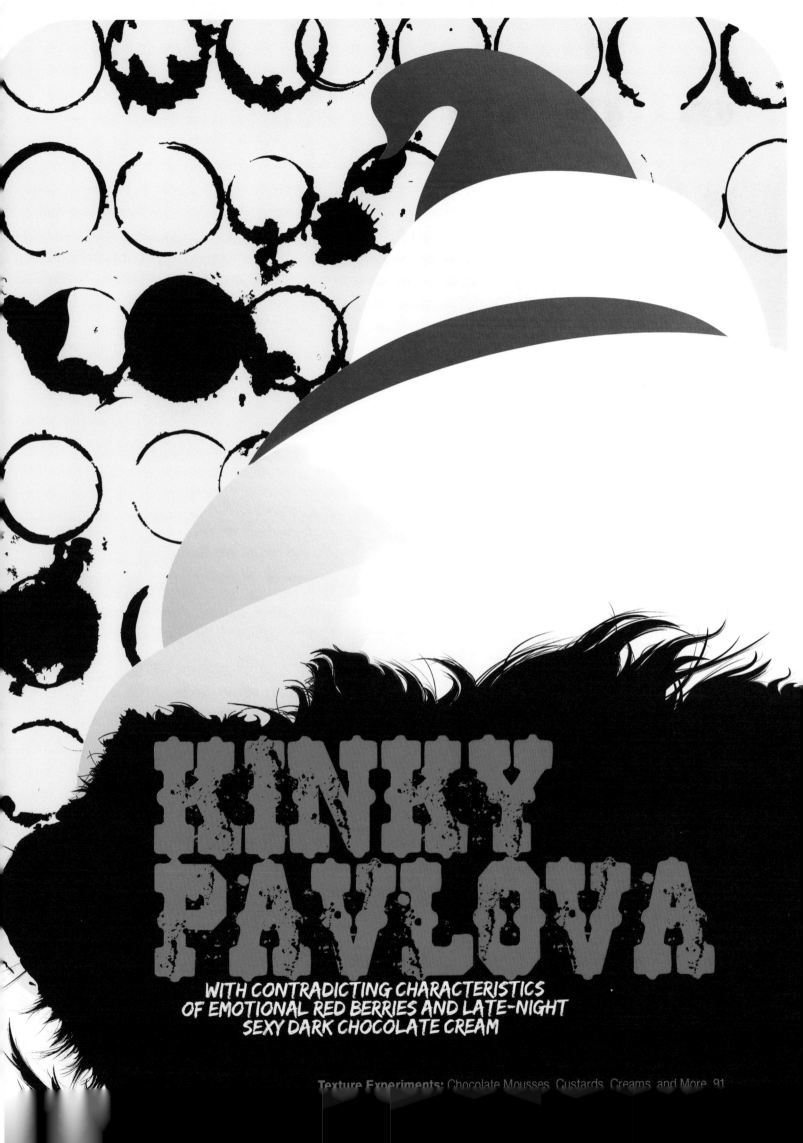

KINKY PAVLOVA

WITH CONTRADICTING CHARACTERISTICS
OF EMOTIONAL RED BERRIES AND LATE-NIGHT
SEXY DARK CHOCOLATE CREAM

Controversial cherry soup

with light brandy musings, snow white chocolate crème fraîche, and a straightforward cinnamon stick

People always tell me that the most important thing in life is knowing how to enjoy the path. But for me, the only truly tasty morsel is the cherry on the icing of the cake.

Cherry Soup

1 (16-ounce) can pitted sour red pie cherries

1 tablespoon granulated sugar

Zest and juice of 1 lemon

2 tablespoons brandy

2 tablespoons orange juice

2 cinnamon sticks

½ cup cold water

1 ½ teaspoons cornstarch, sifted

½ cup crème fraîche

White Chocolate Crème Fraîche

1 cup heavy cream

1 teaspoon confectioners' sugar

1 ½ ounces white chocolate, melted and cooled

1 cup crème fraîche

1. Make the soup. Drain the cherries, pouring the liquid into a medium saucepan and setting the fruit aside.

2. Add the granulated sugar, lemon juice (set the zest aside), brandy, orange juice, and cinnamon sticks to the cherry juice and stir over medium heat until the sugar dissolves.

3. In a small mixing bowl, combine the cold water and cornstarch and mix until smooth. Add to the saucepan. Bring to a boil and simmer, stirring constantly, for 5 minutes, or until the soup thickens. Remove from the heat and chill.

4. When the soup is chilled, whisk in the lemon zest and crème fraîche and add the drained cherries. Chill again before serving.

5. While the soup chills, make the white chocolate crème fraîche. Whip the heavy cream and confectioners' sugar until firm peaks form. Place the cooled white chocolate in a large bowl. Add a dollop of whipped cream and mix to combine. Gently fold the remaining whipped cream into the white chocolate to make a chantilly cream. Fold in the crème fraîche.

6. Serve the chilled soup in chilled cups with dollops of the white chocolate crème fraîche.

Yield: 6 to 8 servings

CONTROVERSIAL CHERRYSOUP

with light brandy musings, snow white chocolate crème fraîche,
and a straightforward cinnamon stick

Tacky double chocolate fondue

made of dark chocolate with a touch of red chili obsession and white chocolate perfumed with soft cherry liqueur

....

Once upon a time I loved you white, the purest and most innocent there is. Later I loved you black: moody and obsessive. But after so many years I love you gray. People say that's the saddest, most boring color of them all, but now I know that I love you mixed black and white, in fact I love you like I've never loved you before.

....

2 cups heavy cream
¼ teaspoon chili powder
¼ teaspoon ground cinnamon
⅛ teaspoon ground nutmeg
9 ounces dark chocolate, chopped
9 ounces white chocolate, chopped
1 tablespoon cherry liqueur

1. Bring 1 cup cream to a boil with the chili powder, cinnamon, and nutmeg. Pour over the dark chocolate in a heatproof bowl and stir until smooth.
2. Bring the remaining 1 cup cream to a boil. Pour over the white chocolate in a heatproof bowl. Add the cherry liqueur. Stir until smooth and set aside.
3. Serve the chocolate sauces in separate bowls placed inside other bowls filled with boiling water, or in bowls over votive candles. This will keep the chocolate hot and melted for about 1 hour.

Recommended for dunking: marshmallows, nuts, soft dry cake, fresh fruits, candied and dried fruits.

Yield: 2 to 4 servings

Tacky
double
chocolate
fondue

made of dark chocolate with a touch
of red chili obsession and white chocolate
perfumed with soft cherry liqueur

All-in-one crackling coconut sugar tortilla chips

with white chocolate and spicy chili milk chocolate guacamole

Chili Milk Chocolate Cream

1 ½ cups heavy cream
10 ounces milk chocolate
Pinch chili powder

Chocolate Guacamole

⅔ cup heavy cream
6 ounces white chocolate, chopped
2 soft avocados, pitted and peeled
⅓ cup granulated sugar
1 tablespoon freshly squeezed lemon juice
5 strawberries, diced

"Tortilla Chips"

1 stick unsalted butter, softened, plus 6 tablespoons
2 cups confectioners' sugar
7 large egg whites, room temperature
2 cups all-purpose flour
2 tablespoons ground hazelnuts
1 cup shredded coconut, lightly toasted

1. Make the chili milk chocolate cream. Bring the cream to a simmer, then pour over the milk chocolate and chili powder in a heatproof bowl. Let sit until the chocolate begins to melt, about 1 minute, then mix until smooth. Chill for 1 hour.

2. Make the chocolate guacamole. Bring the cream to a simmer and pour over the white chocolate in a heatproof bowl. Let sit until the chocolate begins to melt, about 1 minute, then stir until smooth. Let cool.

3. Puree the avocados, granulated sugar, and lemon juice. Add to the white chocolate ganache, mixing until smooth. Gently add the diced strawberries.

4. Make the tortilla chips. Preheat the oven to 325°F. Line a baking sheet with bakers' Silpat. In a large mixing bowl, cream the butter and confectioners' sugar with a handheld mixer. Add the egg whites and continue beating until the mixture is whipped high and fluffy, about 5 minutes. Mix in the flour until just combined. Gently fold in the nuts.

5. Pipe or spoon the egg white mixture onto the prepared sheet in triangles about 2 inches long and ⅕ inch thick. Sprinkle lightly with the toasted coconut. Bake until golden brown, about 7 minutes.

6. Serve a basket of tortilla chips with one bowl of guacamole and one bowl of chili milk chocolate cream.

Yield: 4 servings

ALL-IN-ONE CRACKLING COCONUT SUGAR TORTILLA CHIPS

with white chocolate and spicy chili milk chocolate guacamole

Overwhelming Oriental white chocolate malabi

soothing with feminine rosewater fragrance, roasted coconut, and very sweet deep red cherry lipstick compote

Strong flavors, bold scents, and you across from me with bright red lipstick and endless décolletage all prove to me once again that simplicity is the true ingenuity of the senses.

Ganache

¼ cup heavy cream
1 teaspoon whole cardamom pods
1 cinnamon stick
4 ½ ounces white chocolate, chopped

Malabi

4 cups milk
½ cup cornstarch, sifted
3 tablespoons rosewater
1 ¼ cups heavy cream
½ cup sugar

Cherry Compote

½ pound ripe cherries, pitted
½ cup sugar

Lightly toasted shredded coconut, for serving

1. Make the ganache. Bring the cream to a simmer. Add the cardamom pods and cinnamon stick. Remove from the heat and let the flavors infuse, about 10 minutes.

2. Strain the cream, removing the cardamom pods and cinnamon stick, and bring the cream back to a simmer. Pour over the white chocolate in a heatproof bowl. Let sit until the chocolate begins to melt, about 1 minute, then stir until the ganache is smooth. Pour into the bottom of an 8 to 10-inch glass serving dish and let cool for at least 2 hours in the refrigerator.

3. Make the malabi. Mix 1 cup milk with the cornstarch and rosewater, whisking until the cornstarch dissolves and the mixture is smooth.

4. Combine the remaining 3 cups milk with the cream and sugar in a heavy-bottomed saucepan. Bring to a boil, then whisk in the milk-cornstarch mixture. Boil 3 seconds more, whisking continuously until the mixture thickens. Pour the malabi over the cooled ganache in the glass serving dish. Cover with plastic wrap—the plastic wrap should touch the custard so it does not form a skin. Chill for at least 2 hours before serving.

5. Make the compote. In a heavy-bottomed saucepan, simmer the cherries and sugar together until the cherries are soft. Let cool.

6. Serve the malabi cold with a scoop of cherry compote and a sprinkle of toasted coconut.

Yield: 10 to 12 servings

OVER WHELMING ORIENTAL WHITE CHOCOLATE MALABI
soothing with feminine rosewater fragrance, roasted coconut, and very sweet deep red cherry lipstick compote

A forever toffee apple

coated in tacky red caramel and a white chocolate pine nut silk coat

I will always remember this one beautiful sunny day in the amusement park. I was ten. I asked Dad to give me some money and bought a red toffee apple for the girl who was constantly playing on the white seesaw. Thirty years have passed and I still can't forget her, because when she gave the apple to "Spider" Tom I understood forever that true eternal love is (all) the things I cannot obtain.

6 medium apples (not waxed)
½ stick unsalted butter
2 cups sugar
¼ cup light corn syrup
Zest and juice of 2 oranges
¼ cup heavy cream
4 to 6 drops red food coloring
6 ounces white chocolate, melted
2 cups pine nuts, toasted and chopped

1. Insert the pointed end of a skewer through each apple core, so that it will hold it securely while dipping.

2. Set a wire rack over a parchment-lined baking sheet.

3. Choose a saucepan that is not too wide and has tall sides, as you need to create a "caramel bath" for dipping the apples. In the saucepan with a candy thermometer attached, melt the butter into the sugar, corn syrup, orange zest, and orange juice over high heat. Bring the mixture to a boil and boil, stirring constantly, until the caramel turns a medium golden brown and measures 290°F on the thermometer, about 5 minutes.

4. Reduce the heat and, standing back as the caramel will splatter, slowly add the cream while stirring constantly. Remove from heat and add enough food coloring to achieve a ruby red shade.

5. Dip each apple completely in the caramel. Make sure that the caramel is not cold and the coating is not too thick. If so, reheat briefly. Place the apples on the cooling rack to allow the caramel to drip. When the coating is hard, cut any dripping caramel off with a heated knife.

6. Dip the bottom third of each apple into the melted white chocolate. Chill until the chocolate is mostly hard. Press the toasted pine nuts into the chocolate coating. Serve soon after preparation, so that the caramel coating remains fresh and tasty.

Yield: 6 servings

A FOREVER TOFFEE APPLE

COATED IN TACKY RED CARAMEL AND A WHITE CHOCOLATE PINE NUT SILK COAT

All-the-way confiture of figs

with cocoa nibs, spiritual fresh mint leaves, and immoral vodka

Spiritual and healthy and endlessly innocent or carnal and filled with self-destruction, but never in the middle, only at the contrasting edges: that's the only way to survive.

1 ½ pounds ripe fresh figs
3 ½ to 4 cups sugar
10 fresh mint leaves, chopped
¼ cup vodka, plus more for dipping parchment paper
¼ cup cocoa nibs

1. Cut the figs into 1-inch cubes. Cook in a heavy-bottomed saucepan over low heat until the fruit releases its juices. Add the sugar and mint, and continue cooking over low heat until the mixture thickens, about 30 minutes. Remove a little of the confiture with a spoon, put it on a plate, and check the consistency—it should be jammy. Continue cooking if it is not thick enough.
2. Add the vodka and cook for 3 minutes longer. Mix in the cocoa nibs.
3. Fill four 16-ounce sterilized jam jars with the confiture. Dip rounds of parchment paper in vodka and place on top of the confiture before closing the jars.

Yield: about 4 16-ounce jars

ALL-THE-WAY CONFITURE OF FIGS,

with cocoa nibs, spiritual fresh mint leaves,
and immoral vodka

Unfulfilled candied orange peel

dipped in white chocolate expectations with cardamom and cornflakes

....

In Grandmother's brown wooden cupboard there is a porcelain bonbon dish. On occasion, Grandmother goes to the cupboard, removes it with great ceremony, turns it in her hands, and weighs the possibilities; as always, she decides that once again this is not a good enough reason to use the bonbon dish, which is growing old with disuse, slowly losing its role as the subjective expectation that has never been fulfilled.

....

5 oranges
2 ½ cups sugar, plus more for tossing
1 tablespoon vanilla extract
6 ounces white chocolate, melted
2 cups crushed cornflakes
2 teaspoons ground cardamom

1. Cut the tops and bottoms off the oranges. Using a sharp paring knife, cut the peel away from the fruit in wide strips, about 1 by 2 inches. Set the fruit aside for another use.

2. Fill a large saucepan with water and bring to a boil. Add the orange peels and let boil 2 minutes. Drain and rinse the peels in cold water. Repeat the boil, drain, and rinse process two more times. This will remove any bitterness from the pith.

3. Fill the pot with 4 cups water and add the sugar and vanilla. Bring to a boil and add the peels. Reduce to a simmer, cover, and simmer for 2 hours. Remove from the heat and let sit in the pot, covered, for at least 6 hours or up to overnight. The peels should be soft and completely macerated.

4. Lay the peels out on a cooling rack to dry. Once they are dry, toss in sugar to coat.

5. Mix the melted chocolate with the cornflakes and cardamom. Dip each slice of peel in the chocolate mixture. Chill on a parchment-lined baking sheet for at least 30 minutes before serving.

Yield: 10 servings

UNFULFILLED CANDIED ORANGE PEEL

DIPPED IN WHITE CHOCOLATE EXPECTATIONS

WITH CARDAMOM AND CORNFLAKES

Bad boy chocolate pizza

with hazelnut spread, pure melted chocolate chips, and passionately roasted marshmallows

I observe, without moving a muscle, the focused sensuality in front of me until the point of bursting. The more I want to eat, the less I want to eat . . . I want to revel in the lust, I want to make love to it and never ever fail to taste the passion, the infinite essence of life . . .

Pizza Dough (recipe follows) or 1 pound store-bought
    pizza dough
2 teaspoons unsalted butter, melted
¼ cup chocolate-hazelnut spread (recommended:
    Nutella)
½ cup semisweet chocolate chips
½ ounce milk chocolate chips
½ ounce white chocolate chips
1 cup chopped large marshmallows or miniature
    marshmallows

1. Position the oven rack on the bottom of the oven and preheat to 450°F. Line a large baking sheet with parchment paper.
2. Roll the dough into a 9-inch round. Transfer to the prepared baking sheet. Using your fingers, make indentations all over the dough. Brush with the melted butter. Bake until the crust is crisp and pale golden brown, about 20 minutes.
3. Immediately spread the chocolate-hazelnut spread over the pizza, then sprinkle with the chocolate chips and marshmallows. Bake until the chocolate just begins to melt, about 2 minutes. Cut the pizza into wedges and serve.

Yield: 8 to 10 servings

Pizza Dough
½ cup water
1 envelope dry yeast
2 cups all-purpose flour, plus more for kneading
1 teaspoon salt
3 tablespoons unsalted butter, melted, plus more
    for bowl

1. Heat the water to 110°F. In a small bowl, mix the warm water and yeast. Let stand until the yeast dissolves, about 5 minutes. In a food processor, blend the flour and salt. With the machine running, slowly add the melted butter and then the yeast mixture. Mix until the dough just comes together.
2. On a lightly floured surface, knead the dough, adding more flour if necessary, until smooth, about 1 minute. Transfer the dough to a large buttered bowl, turning once so the butter coats the dough. Cover with a clean kitchen towel and set aside in a warm, draft-free place until the dough doubles in volume, about 1 hour. Punch the dough down and form into a ball. The dough can be used immediately or stored airtight in the refrigerator for 1 day.

Yield: enough dough to make one 9-inch pizza

bad boy
chocolate
pizza

with hazelnut spread, pure melted
chocolate chips and passionately
roasted marshmallows

The adult and child chocolate burger joint venture

with Bloody Mary strawberry ketchup and hazelnut vanilla cream mustard

. . . .

"Burgers"

1 ½ cups heavy cream
Pinch black pepper
15 ounces dark chocolate, chopped
2 tablespoons aged brown rum
Pinch sea salt

Hazelnut Vanilla Cream "Mustard"

⅓ cup milk
6 ounces white chocolate, chopped
⅓ cup roasted hazelnuts, chopped

Bloody Mary Strawberry "Ketchup"

3 tablespoons hot water
¼ cup sugar
2 cups strawberries, hulled and mashed
Juice of 1 lemon
1 tablespoon vodka
3 drops Tabasco sauce
5 hamburger buns
15 marshmallows

1. Make the burgers. Bring the cream to a simmer and add the pepper. Pour over the dark chocolate in a heatproof bowl. Let sit until the chocolate begins to melt, about 1 minute, then add the rum and salt and stir until smooth.

2. Place five 4-inch metal rings on a baking sheet lined with parchment paper. Pour the chocolate cream into the rings to form the burgers (¾ inch high). Chill until hard, at least 2 hours.

3. Make the vanilla mustard. Bring the milk to a simmer and pour over the white chocolate in a heatproof bowl. Let sit until the chocolate begins to soften, about 1 minute, then stir until smooth. Mix in the chopped hazelnuts.

4. Make the ketchup. Simmer the water and sugar until the sugar dissolves. Let cool. Pour the syrup into a cocktail shaker and add the mashed strawberries, lemon juice, vodka, and Tabasco. Shake until well combined.

5. Preheat the broiler to high. Place the bun tops on a broiler pan, cut side up. Place the marshmallows on the buns. Broil until the marshmallow is golden brown and melting, 2 to 3 minutes.

6. Spread the vanilla mustard and ketchup on the bottom buns. Top with a chocolate hamburger and cover with the top buns. Serve immediately.

Yield: 5 servings

THE ADULT
and child CHOCOLATE
BURGER
joint venture

with Bloody Mary
strawberry ketchup
and hazelnut vanilla
cream mustard

Unforgettable punch banana ice cream

with a touch of piña colada, Calvados, and a boost of serious chocolate memorable cream

A small boy in an ice cream parlor faced with the endless variety of flavors and aromas must select only one and remember forever and ever the wondrous taste of the flavor he did *not* choose, the relentlessly nagging taste of an opportunity you lose.

Ganache
¼ cup heavy cream
4 ½ ounces dark chocolate, chopped
1 teaspoon banana liqueur

Ice Cream
6 large egg yolks
Scant ½ cup sugar
1 ¼ cups heavy cream
3 ripe bananas, sliced
2 tablespoons piña colada mix (or substitute 2
    tablespoons cream of coconut)
8 strawberries, hulled and lightly mashed with the back
    of a wooden spoon
2 tablespoons Calvados

1. Line a loaf pan with 2 pieces of plastic wrap (at right angles to each other) so that plastic wrap hangs over all 4 sides of the pan. Place the pan in the freezer to chill while you prepare the ganache and ice cream.
2. Make the ganache. Bring the cream to a simmer and pour over the chocolate in a heatproof bowl. Add the liqueur. Let sit until the chocolate begins to melt, about 1 minute, then stir until smooth. Pour the chocolate into the prepared loaf pan, spreading evenly along the bottom. Return the pan to the freezer.
3. Make the ice cream. In a large heatproof mixing bowl set over simmering water (a bain-marie), whisk together the egg yolks and sugar. Whisk continuously so the eggs don't have a chance to scramble, until the mixture turns pale yellow and doubles in volume, about 5 minutes. It should resemble thick yellow cake batter. Remove from the heat and keep whisking until cool.

4. In the bowl of a standing mixer fitted with a whisk attachment, whip the cream until firm peaks form. Loosen the yolk mixture with a dollop of the whipped cream, then fold in the remaining cream. Divide the ice cream base evenly between 2 bowls.
5. In a small bowl, combine the banana slices and piña colada mix, mashing lightly together to blend the flavors. Do the same with the strawberries and Calvados in a separate bowl.
6. Gently fold the banana mixture into one bowl of the ice cream base, then pour into the bottom of the loaf pan. Gently fold the strawberry mixture into the remaining ice cream base and pour on top of the banana layer. Fold the plastic wrap flaps over the top of the ice cream. Freeze overnight.
7. Let the ice cream soften at room temperature for several minutes before serving. Invert onto a serving platter, then slice.

Yield: 8 servings

Unforgettable
Punch Banana Ice cream
with a touch of piña colada, Calvados, and a boost
of serious chocolate memorable cream

Banana split

with caramel disco, chocolate punk sauce, and roasted macadamia minimalism

The twenties, the forties, the eighties . . . welcome to the retro shop. You'll find on the shelf an instant personality formula look. Prêt à pretend. Choose today's worst seller: a guarantee to become immediately the number one, the hottest talk of the town.

1 stick unsalted butter
1 ½ cups sugar
1 teaspoon salt
1 ¼ cups heavy cream
3 ounces dark chocolate chips
4 ripe but firm bananas, peeled
8 scoops vanilla ice cream

½ cup macadamia nuts, toasted and chopped

1. Melt the butter with the sugar and salt in a heavy-bottomed saucepan. Bring to a boil and simmer until the mixture is thick and dark golden brown. Remove from the heat, add the cream, and stir constantly until smooth. Add the chocolate chips and let sit until the chocolate begins to melt, about 1 minute. Stir until the mixture is smooth. Let cool until thickened, about 5 minutes.
2. Cut each banana in half lengthwise and place in an oblong dish. Add 2 scoops of ice cream to the middle of each, pour the caramel chocolate sauce on top, and sprinkle with the macadamia nuts.

Yield: 4 servings

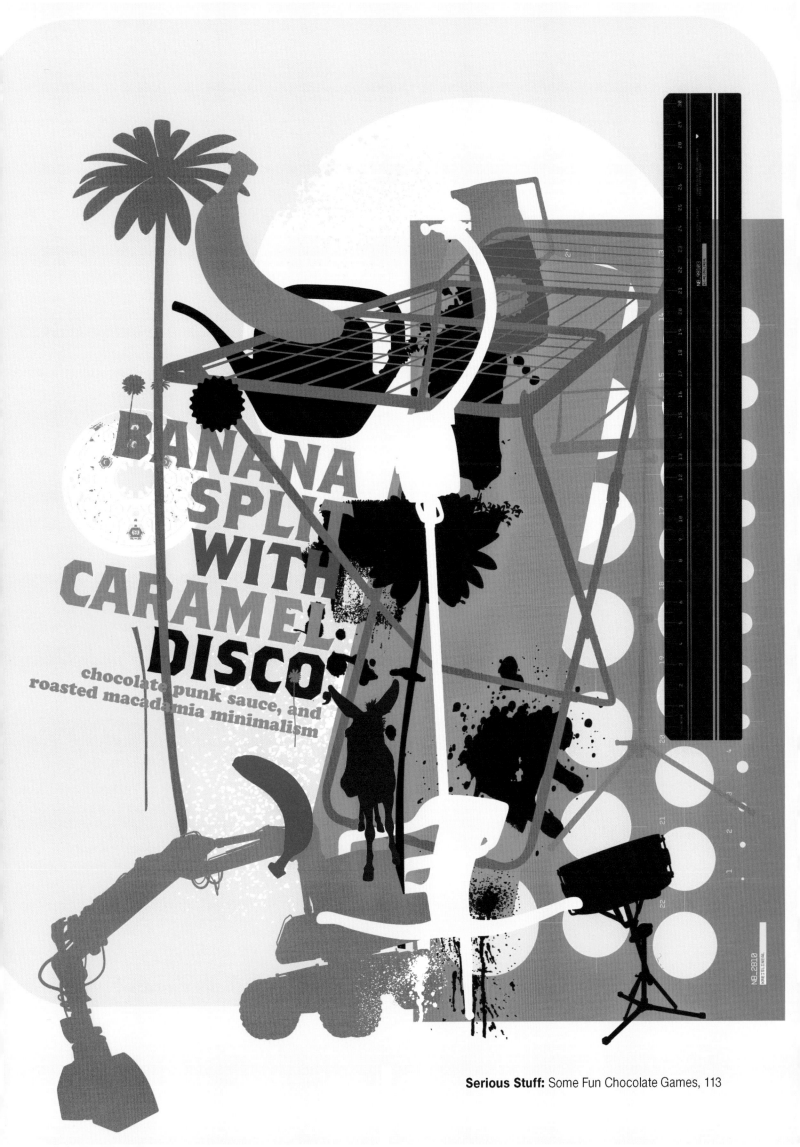

BANANA SPLIT WITH CARAMEL DISCO: chocolate punk sauce, and roasted macadamia minimalism

Innocent meringue kisses

with edges dipped in magical chocolate and served with passion fruit reality

....

When I was five, I fell in love with Snow White. Twenty years later I was living in Paris. Then, for the first time in my life, I met her. She came for only an hour. We lit candles and I put on the music I always wanted to listen to with her. She didn't say a word, but in her beautiful silent way she made me understand that my legendary love will work its magic with any other ordinary girl in the world.

....

4 large egg whites
½ cup granulated sugar
½ cup confectioners' sugar, plus more for dusting
¼ teaspoon salt
⅛ teaspoon almond extract
7 ½ ounces dark chocolate, roughly chopped
Pulp of 10 passion fruits

1. Preheat the oven to 200°F. Line large baking sheets with parchment paper or bakers' Silpat.
2. Using a hand mixer or the whisk attachment of a standing mixer, beat the egg whites until frothy. Continue beating while slowly adding the granulated sugar and then the confectioners' sugar and salt. Continue beating until soft peaks form. Add the almond extract and continue beating until the whites are glossy and hold stiff peaks.
3. Gently spoon the egg whites into a pastry bag fitted with a round tip or a plastic bag with a corner cut. Using a gentle squeezing motion, pipe the meringue out on the prepared sheets in kiss shapes, about 1 inch in diameter.
4. Bake the meringue kisses for 2 hours, then turn the oven off without opening the oven door—doing so will let humid air inside, and the meringues won't dry out. Let the meringues dry in the oven for at least 3 hours or overnight.
5. When the meringues are dry, melt the dark chocolate and let sit until completely cool. Dip one side of each meringue in the melted chocolate and set to dry on parchment paper or a cooling rack. Dust lightly with sifted confectioners' sugar and serve with passion fruit pulp.

Yield: about 60 small meringue kisses

INNOCENT MERINGUE KISSES

WITH EDGES DIPPED IN MAGICAL CHOCOLATE AND SERVED WITH PASSION FRUIT REALITY

Meaningless sweet spaghetti

with my one and only chocolate ganache, fruit, and incomparable Irish Cream

A hot chocolate sauce made sometime earlier was spilled into the pedigreed chef's bowl of spaghetti. Now he must explain this stroke of good luck; no doubt his mixture of scrambled words will be crowned "genius" with verve and pluck!

1 ½ pounds spaghetti
¾ cup heavy cream
1 teaspoon Irish Cream liqueur
Juice of 1 orange
7 ½ ounces dark chocolate, roughly chopped
12 strawberries, sliced
Toasted pecans, to taste
Toasted pistachios, to taste

1. Prepare the spaghetti according to the package directions.
2. While the spaghetti cooks, bring the cream to a simmer over medium heat. Whisk in the Irish Cream and orange juice, then pour over the chopped chocolate in a large heatproof bowl. Let sit until the chocolate begins to melt, about 1 minute, then whisk into a smooth chocolate ganache.
3. Drain the cooked spaghetti, then toss with the chocolate ganache. Top with strawberries and toasted nuts and serve immediately.

Yield: 6 to 8 servings

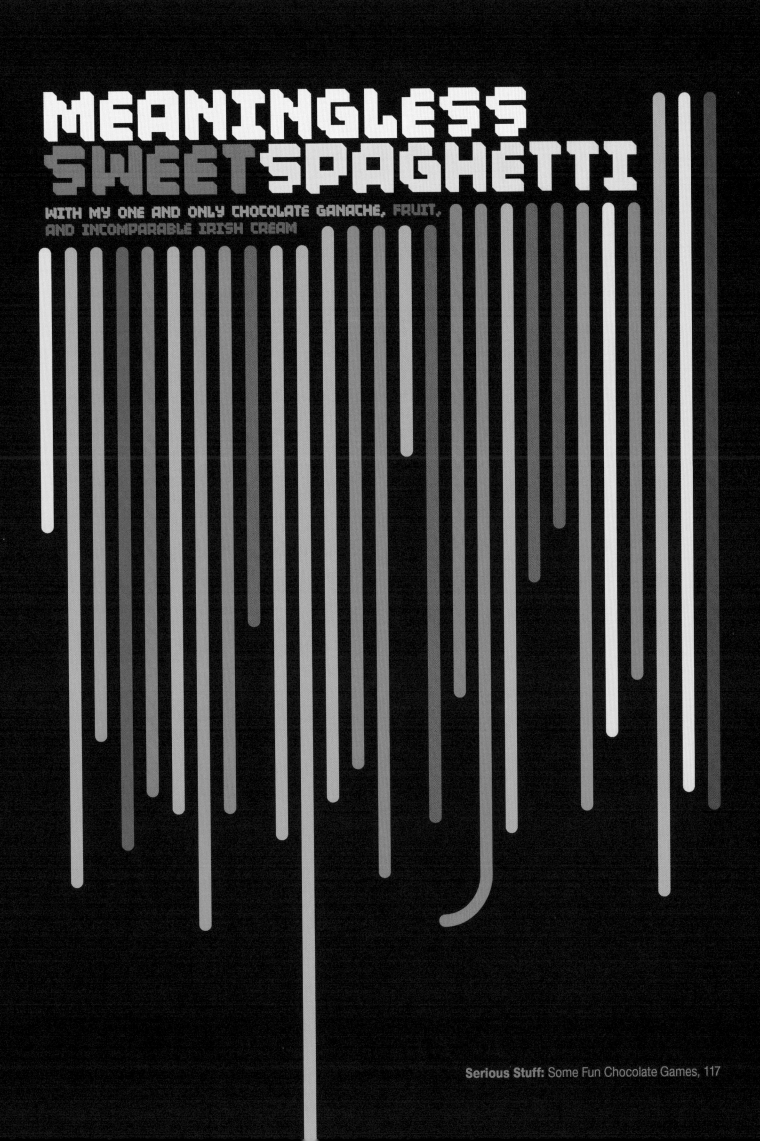

MEANINGLESS SWEET SPAGHETTI

WITH MY ONE AND ONLY CHOCOLATE GANACHE, FRUIT,
AND INCOMPARABLE IRISH CREAM

Home industry chocolate cheese pockets

filled with pears cooked in wine and made according to a cheesy chef's recipe

Poached Pears

2 ½ cups sugar

2 ½ cups water

4 firm pears, peeled and finely diced

¾ cup good-quality white wine

Dough

5 ½ cups all-purpose flour

1 large egg plus 1 large egg yolk

½ teaspoon salt

1 envelope dry yeast

3 tablespoons warm milk

2 ½ sticks unsalted butter, softened

⅓ cup sugar

Cheese Filling

2 ½ cups milk

⅓ cup sugar

4 tablespoons cornstarch, sifted

5 large egg yolks

¾ cup mascarpone cheese

12 ounces milk chocolate, chopped

Egg Wash

1 large egg yolk

2 tablespoons water

Confectioners' sugar for dusting

1. Poach the pears. Simmer the sugar and water until the sugar dissolves. Remove from the heat. Stir in the pears and wine. Let cool. Chill for at least 12 hours. Drain and dry the pears completely. Set aside.

2. Make the dough. In a large bowl, mix together the flour, egg and egg yolk, and salt. In a separate bowl combine the yeast and warm milk and stir until the yeast dissolves. Add to the flour mixture. Beat in the butter and sugar. Knead into a smooth dough, about 5 minutes. Cover and let rest in the refrigerator for at least 2 hours.

3. On a lightly floured work surface, roll the dough into a 20-inch square about ¼ inch thick. Cut into sixteen 5 by 5-inch squares.

4. Make the cheese filling. Bring the milk to a boil in a heavy-bottomed saucepan. Set aside. In a heatproof bowl, mix the sugar, cornstarch, and egg yolks. Pour some milk into the bowl, then pour this mixture back into the remaining milk in the saucepan and bring to a boil again, for 30 seconds, while stirring. Let the mixture cool to room temperature and mix in the mascarpone.

5. Preheat the oven to 350°F. Line 2 baking sheets with parchment paper.

6. Spread a thick layer of the cheese mixture across the end of each piece of dough. Sprinkle with pears and chopped chocolate. Fold the other half of the dough over the filling and pinch all sides to seal.

7. Place the pockets on the prepared baking sheets. Mix the yolk and water together to create an egg wash. Lightly brush the pockets with the egg wash. Bake until golden brown, about 25 minutes, then sprinkle with confectioners' sugar. Serve hot.

Yield: 15 pockets

HOME INDUSTRY CHOCOLATE CHEESE POCKETS

filled with **PEARS COOKED IN WINE**

and made according to a cheesy chef's recipe

Jealous almond and pistachio marzipan balls

with Grand Marnier and hazelnut centers, coated in satanic dark chocolate

The reception hall is completely full. The door opens and the crowd rises to its feet, applauding him. He played so well today and made such beautiful music. Bottles of champagne are opened. Waiters pass through the room with golden trays laden with pyramids of marzipan balls. The bitterness of their almonds mixed devoutly with the sweetness of the sugar is the perfect analogy to the desperate war raging in my heart due to the close friendship we share: the war between the sweetness of my affection for him and the bitter jealousy with which I pray in utmost sincerity for him to fail.

1 cup plus 1 pinch granulated sugar
1 cup water
½ cup blanched almonds
½ cup shelled pistachios
2 tablespoons Grand Marnier
Confectioners' sugar, for dusting
20 to 25 hazelnuts
3 ounces dark chocolate, melted

1. Make a simple syrup by bringing 1 cup granulated sugar and the water to a boil in a heavy-bottomed saucepan. Boil until the sugar is dissolved and syrup has thickened, 8 to 10 minutes. Remove from the heat.

2. In the bowl of a food processor, blitz the almonds, pistachios, and the pinch granulated sugar into a fine powder. Add the Grand Marnier.

3. Make the marzipan. With the food processor running, slowly add some simple syrup to the nut mixture, adding only enough so the nuts form a smooth paste. How much you use will depend on the humidity of the day, so add slowly and don't worry if you use only half the syrup. Cover the mixture and chill overnight.

4. Divide the marzipan into 20 to 25 pieces. Place on a baking sheet lined with parchment paper. Dust your hands with confectioners' sugar, then use your thumb to press one whole hazelnut deep into the center of each ball. Gently roll the ball so the marzipan completely surrounds the hazelnut.

5. Roll each ball in the melted dark chocolate, then set on parchment paper to dry. Dust lightly with confectioners' sugar before serving.

Yield: 20 to 25 pieces

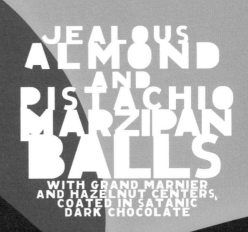

JEALOUS
ALMOND
AND
PISTACHIO
MARZIPAN
BALLS
WITH GRAND MARNIER
AND HAZELNUT CENTERS,
COATED IN SATANIC
DARK CHOCOLATE

Well-disciplined ladyfingers

dipped in milk chocolate therapy, pistachios and roasted coconut

You know, Mommy, I am fifty today. I still clean my plate. The doctor says I have to change my eating habits, otherwise I am at risk of having a stroke. Is it more dangerous than having a lifetime education breakdown?

6 large egg whites plus 4 large egg yolks

1 tablespoon plus ½ cup granulated sugar

3 tablespoons all-purpose flour

¼ teaspoon salt

Juice of ½ lemon

1 teaspoon vanilla extract

6 ounces milk chocolate, melted

1 cup shelled pistachios, finely chopped

7 ounces flaked coconut (about 2 cups), lightly toasted

Confectioners' sugar, for dusting

1. Preheat the oven to 350°F. Line large baking sheets with bakers' Silpat or lightly buttered wax paper.

2. In a large bowl, combine the egg whites and 1 tablespoon sugar. Using an electric mixer, beat the whites into glossy stiff peaks. Set aside.

3. In a small bowl, sift together the flour and salt. In a large bowl, whisk together the yolks and remaining ½ cup sugar, beating until pale yellow and thickened to the consistency of cake batter, about 5 minutes. Beat in the lemon juice and vanilla. Using a rubber spatula, gently fold the flour mixture into the yolk mixture until just combined.

4. Gently fold the egg whites into the yolk mixture, mixing until just combined. The mixture will be somewhat frothy and voluminous.

5. Spoon the batter into a large pastry bag fitted with a ½-inch round tip. Pipe batter onto the prepared sheets to form the traditional ladyfinger shape (about 4 ½ inches long). Bake until puffy and golden brown, about 10 minutes. Remove from oven and let cool.

6. Dip the top of a cooled ladyfinger into the melted chocolate and set on a cooling rack. Sprinkle chocolate with chopped pistachios and coconut. Repeat with the remaining ladyfingers. Decorate with confectioners' sugar.

Yield: about 3 dozen ladyfingers

WELL-DISCIPLINED LADYFINGERS

dipped in milk chocolate therapy, pistachios and roasted coconut

No.

Once-upon-a-time small almond cookies

with a long-ago sound of crackling sugar edges dipped in milk chocolate nostalgia

···

An unforgettable taste sampled many years ago becomes impossible in one's imagination, an obsessive yearning, an endless search, and every new sampling full of promise turns into, as always, the taste of disappointment.

···

2 ½ sticks unsalted butter, softened
1 ¾ cups sugar, plus more for sprinkling
2 large eggs
2 teaspoons vanilla extract
2 ¾ cups all-purpose flour
1 teaspoon salt
1 teaspoon baking soda
1 ½ teaspoons ground cinnamon
¼ teaspoon ground nutmeg
1 cup almonds, finely ground
6 ounces milk chocolate, chopped

1. Using a hand mixer or the paddle attachment of a standing mixer, cream the butter and sugar together until light and fluffy, about 3 minutes. Mix in the eggs one by one. Mix in the vanilla.

2. In a separate bowl sift together the flour, salt, baking soda, ½ teaspoon cinnamon, and the nutmeg. Stir in the ground almonds.

3. With the mixer on slow, gradually add the dry ingredients to the wet until thoroughly incorporated. Wrap the dough in plastic and chill in the refrigerator for at least 1 hour.

4. Preheat the oven to 350°F. Line 2 large baking sheets with parchment paper or bakers' Silpat.

5. Drop the dough by rounded tablespoons onto the sheets, spacing them 1 ½ inches apart as the cookies will spread while baking. Sprinkle lightly with sugar. Bake until thin, lacy, and golden brown, about 8 minutes. Remove from the oven and let cool completely as cookies will need to harden before dipping.

6. When the cookies are cool, melt the milk chocolate with the remaining 1 teaspoon cinnamon. Dip half of each cookie in the warm chocolate and set to dry on parchment paper.

Yield: about 30 cookies

Once-upon-a-time
SMALL ALMOND COOKIES
with a long-ago sound of crackling sugar edges dipped in milk chocolate nostalgia

Contentious chocolate chip cookies

filled with all the world's goodies

When the devil's craving for fresh cookies crawls up the tiny veins in your head, don't ever listen to your inner advocate, who gives an inspiring speech on "self-control and the cookie jar." Just give in and behave as if all the great achievements of humankind have been fulfilled: go for it all the way . . . enjoy!

2 sticks unsalted butter, softened
1 ¼ cups packed brown sugar
2 large eggs
1 ½ teaspoons vanilla extract
2 cups all-purpose flour
1 teaspoon salt
1 teaspoon baking soda
½ teaspoon ground cinnamon
¼ teaspoon ground nutmeg
¼ teaspoon ground cloves
½ cup chopped walnuts
Scant ½ cup chopped dried apricots
¼ cup candied orange peel
3 ounces milk chocolate chips or chopped milk chocolate
3 ounces dark chocolate chips or chopped dark chocolate

1. Using a hand mixer or standing mixer fitted with a paddle attachment, cream the butter and sugar until light and fluffy. Add the eggs one by one, mixing well after each addition. Add the vanilla.

2. In a separate bowl, sift the flour, salt, baking soda, cinnamon, nutmeg, and cloves together. Stir in the walnuts. Slowly add the dry ingredients to the butter mixture, mixing until thoroughly incorporated. Mix in the apricots and candied orange peel, followed by the milk and dark chocolates.

3. Wrap the dough in plastic and chill for at least an hour, or roll into a log and wrap in wax paper and freeze overnight.

4. Preheat the oven to 350°F. Line baking sheets with parchment or bakers' Silpat. Drop tablespoons of the dough or place slices of frozen dough on the prepared baking sheets. Bake until golden brown, about 9 minutes. Let cool on the sheet for a few minutes, then transfer to a wire rack to cool completely.

Yield: about 28 cookies

CONTENTIOUS
CHOCOLATE
CHIP COOKIES
FILLED WITH ALL THE
WORLD'S GOODIES

A Nostalgic Homage: The Chocolate Cookie Jar, 127

Wannabe French hot chocolate

served in a soup bowl and topped with creamy hopes

....

Paris. Coffee shops with pictures of Dalí, Sartre, and Jacques Brel on the walls. Beautiful girls on bikes. It is raining and I just bought an old quill pen and a hardcover notebook, but I definitely will not write now, since the book I will start tomorrow is so much better than the book I would write today.

....

2 tablespoons cornstarch, sifted

3 ½ cups milk

½ cup sugar

2 large egg yolks

1 vanilla bean, split lengthwise, or 1 teaspoon vanilla
    extract

7 ounces semisweet chocolate, chopped

1 cup heavy cream, whipped

Unsweetened cocoa powder for sprinkling

1. Sprinkle the cornstarch over ½ cup milk in a small bowl and whisk to dissolve. Whisk in the sugar and egg yolks until combined.

2. In a heavy-bottomed saucepan over low heat, bring 2 cups milk and the vanilla bean to a gentle simmer. (If using extract, add it below.) Remove the bean, scrape the vanilla seeds into the milk, and discard the bean. Gradually whisk the warm milk into the egg yolk mixture, then return the mixture to the pan.

3. Cook, whisking often, until the mixture comes to a full boil, about 3 minutes. If using vanilla extract, stir it in now. Strain the custard through a wire sieve into a bowl.

4. Add the chocolate to the custard. Bring the remaining 1 cup milk to a boil and pour over the custard and chocolate mixture. Let sit until chocolate begins to melt, about 1 minute, then stir until smooth.

5. Add any flavoring you desire—raspberry syrup, cinnamon, holiday spice, marshmallows, etc. You can also substitute white, dark, or milk chocolate for the semisweet. Pour the thick chocolate into mugs and enjoy a generous dollop of whipped cream. Sprinkle with cocoa powder.

Yield: 6 servings

Wannabe French hot chocolate

SERVED IN A SOUP BOWL
AND TOPPED WITH CREAMY HOPES

PARIS

Shanti white chocolate chai image

and spicy moneymaking cookie hope

½ cup whole milk
12 ounces white chocolate, chopped
4 chai tea bags
2 cups boiling-hot water
Sakori Cookies (recipe follows)

1. Bring the milk to a boil. Pour over the chocolate in a heatproof bowl. Let sit until the chocolate begins to soften, about 1 minute, then stir until smooth.
2. Steep the tea bags in the boiling water for 4 minutes. Discard the tea bags and whisk the chocolate milk into the tea. Serve immediately.

Yield: 4 servings

Sakori Cookies
2 cups ground hazelnuts
2 cups ground walnuts
2 cups sugar
4 large egg whites
Pinch five-spice powder

1. Line 3 large baking sheets with parchment paper or bakers' Silpat. Preheat the oven to 325°F.
2. In a medium pot fitted with a candy thermometer, stir all the ingredients together over a low flame until the mixture reaches 105°F. Use a teaspoon to scoop small rounds from the mixture and place on the prepared baking sheets. Bake until golden brown, about 15 minutes. Let cool and serve with white chocolate chai.

Yield: about 60 cookies

Shanti
white
chocolate
chai
image

and spicy
moneymaking
cookie hope

Colorful milkshake

made of white chocolate desires, strawberry passion and fresh yogurt ambitions

....

As on every Friday, I cycle over to Baum's ice cream parlor. But this time I do not stop, will never stop again. I keep pedaling, riding madly on in order to prove to you over and over and forever the enormity of your mistake, when you hung out with him after you'd told me you were busy and that our turn would be next.

....

10 fresh mint leaves
1 cup milk
¼ cup sugar
1 ½ ounces white chocolate, chopped
3 cups fresh strawberries, hulled
½ cup plain low-fat yogurt
30 ice cubes
5 small scoops vanilla ice cream

1. Bring the mint, milk, and sugar to a boil in a small saucepan. Remove from the heat and let infuse 10 minutes.
2. Remove and discard the mint leaves. Add the chocolate to the milk. Let sit until the chocolate begins to melt, about 1 minute, then stir until smooth. If chocolate doesn't melt, briefly return the pan to the heat. Cool to room temperature.
3. Place the strawberries in a high-speed blender and blend to a pulp. Add the white chocolate cream, yogurt, and ice cubes and blend until smooth. Increase the amount of ice cubes if you wish to obtain more of a granita-like texture. Serve in tall glasses with dollops of ice cream on top.

Yield: 5 servings

COLORFUL MILKSHAKE

made of white chocolate desires,
strawberry passion and fresh
yogurt ambitions

The eternal chocolate bliss Indian lassi

with Shiva's 21st-century organic chocolate barfi

An explosion of healthy vitamins. Eighteen hours of work, traffic jams, nonstop information bombarding our brains. Hectic life. But don't we live the real simplicity? Balancing formulas are easy to get, easy to digest, instant Ganges nirvana.

1 cup water
10 fresh mint leaves
1-inch piece fresh ginger, peeled and finely grated
5 cloves
2 mangoes, peeled and pitted
20 ice cubes
1 ½ ounces organic white chocolate chips
¾ cup plain yogurt
Scant 3 tablespoons honey
Juice of 1 lemon
Organic Milk Chocolate Barfi (recipe follows)

1. Boil the water with the mint leaves, ginger, and cloves. Remove from heat and chill for at least 1 hour.
2. Strain the chilled water into the bowl of a blender. Discard the solids. Add the mangoes, ice, white chocolate, yogurt, honey, and lemon juice to the blender and blend well. Serve very cold with the barfi.

Yield: 4 servings

Organic Milk Chocolate Barfi
1 (15-ounce) container ricotta cheese
1 stick unsalted butter
¾ cup sugar
2 cups nonfat powdered milk
¼ cup almonds, lightly ground
1 ½ ounces organic milk chocolate chips
½ teaspoon ground cardamom
6 sheets edible silver foil

1. Line a 9 x 13-inch pan with aluminum foil.
2. Combine the ricotta and butter in a large saucepan over medium-low heat. Cook, stirring occasionally to keep the cheese from burning, until the mixture is wet and homogenous, about 20 minutes.
3. Stir in the sugar and powdered milk and cook until the ricotta has a fudge-like consistency, about 5 minutes. Stir in the almonds, milk chocolate, and cardamom. Pour the cheese mixture into the prepared baking pan, using a spatula to spread the mixture evenly. Let cool slightly.
4. Decorate with edible foil and cut into desired shapes for serving. Cover and refrigerate any remaining pieces for up to 5 days.

Yield: 10 servings

THE ETERNAL CHOCOLATE BLISS INDIAN LASSI WITH SHIVA'S 21st-CENTURY ORGANIC CHOCOLATE BARFI

Consensus American chocolate cookie shake

with a cookie inspiration from the all-time original

1 ⅔ cups whole milk
12 ounces white chocolate, chopped
4 chocolate sandwich cookies, crushed
4 cups ice
8 honey-roasted pecans
Cocoa Cookies (recipe follows)

1. Bring 1 cup milk to a boil. Pour over the chocolate in a heatproof bowl. Let sit until the chocolate begins to melt, about 1 minute, then stir until smooth. Cover and chill for at least 2 hours.
2. Add the white chocolate mixture to a blender along with the remaining ⅔ cup milk, the cookies, ice, and pecans. Blend until smooth. Pour into tall frosty glasses and serve immediately.

Yield: 5 servings

Cocoa Cookies

1 ¾ sticks unsalted butter
2 ½ cups flour
2 tablespoons unsweetened cocoa powder, sifted
½ cup granulated sugar
1 large egg
2 cups heavy cream
⅓ cup confectioners' sugar

1. Using an electric mixer, beat the butter, flour, and cocoa powder until sandy in texture. Add the granulated sugar and egg and continue mixing until the dough is smooth and comes together. Cover and let rest in the refrigerator for at least 1 hour.
2. Preheat the oven to 325°F. Line 2 baking sheets with parchment paper or bakers' Silpat.
3. On a lightly floured work surface, pound the dough until it is ¼ inch thick. Using a cookie cutter or shot glass, cut the dough into 1 ¼-inch circles and place on the lined baking sheets. Bake until golden brown, about 20 minutes. Cool completely.
4. Whip the cream and confectioners' sugar until it forms firm peaks. Spread a generous layer of cream on a baked, cooled cookie. Sandwich with another cookie on top. Enjoy with the cookie shake.

Yield: about 30 cookie sandwiches

CONSISTENCY

CONSISTENT

SUS

with a cookie inspiration from the all-time original

AMERICAN
CHOCOLATE COOKIE
SHAKE

Frozen very hot margaritas

with lychees, tempting mandarin vodka, and a salty chocolate peanut brittle fantasy

We're sitting at the bar, it's dark, and everyone is crammed together. Last drink, and I inhale you deep inside me and, as on every evening, plunder your scent without permission according to a pre-planned imperative, and sell myself a precious dream that cannot be realistically assessed.

30 ice cubes
20 lychees, shelled and seeded
½ cup tequila
¼ cup mandarin vodka
Juice of 2 limes, freshly squeezed
Salty Chocolate Peanut Brittle (recipe follows),
    for serving

Place the ice, lychees, tequila, vodka, and lime juice in a blender and blend until smooth. Serve with pieces of the peanut brittle.

Yield: 3 to 4 servings

Salty Chocolate Peanut Brittle
2 sticks unsalted butter
2 cups sugar
2 cups salted roasted peanuts, plus more for topping
6 ounces milk chocolate, chopped
Good-quality sea salt, to taste

1. Line a baking sheet with lightly buttered parchment paper and set aside on a heatproof surface.
2. In a heavy-bottomed saucepan with a candy thermometer attached, melt the butter and sugar. Bring to a boil over medium heat, stirring occasionally with a heatproof spatula. Continue stirring until the mixture is golden brown and measures 300°F on the thermometer.
3. Careful so as not to splatter, stir in the peanuts. Pour the mixture onto the prepared baking sheet, using the spatula to spread the toffee evenly over the paper.
4. Let the brittle harden 1 minute before topping with the milk chocolate. Let the chocolate melt, about 1 minute, then spread to coat the brittle.
5. Sprinkle with sea salt and more peanuts. Chill at least 45 minutes before serving.

Yield: 12 servings

FROZEN
VERY HOT
MARGARITAS

WITH LYCHEES, TEMPTING MANDARIN
VODKA, AND A SALTY CHOCOLATE PEANUT
BRITTLE FANTASY.

Anonymous white chocolate cosmopolitans

in the famous martini glass from The TV Series, served with a touristy wasabi chocolate peanut cluster

∙∙

¼ cup whole milk
7 ounces white chocolate, chopped
1 ¾ cups vodka
¾ cup Cointreau
 1 cup cranberry juice
Juice of 1 lemon
Chocolate-covered Peanuts (recipe follows)

∙∙

1. Bring the milk to a boil, then pour it over the chocolate in a heatproof bowl. Cover and let sit until the chocolate begins to melt, about 1 minute. Whisk until smooth. Set aside until cool, about 20 minutes.
2. Pour the chocolate mixture into a cocktail shaker with ice. Add the vodka, Cointreau, cranberry juice, and lemon juice. Shake well and serve in tall glasses.

Yield: 5 servings

Chocolate-covered Peanuts

1 pinch wasabi powder
2 cups dark chocolate, chopped
45 salted peanuts

∙∙

1. Line a baking sheet with wax paper or bakers' Silpat.
2. Mix the wasabi powder with 1 teaspoon water. Stir until smooth.
3. Melt the chocolate in a heatproof mixing bowl set over simmering water (a bain-marie) or in a bowl in the microwave. Remove from heat and stir in the wasabi. Dip 3 peanuts at a time in the chocolate and place on the baking sheet. Refrigerate until cold, at least 2 hours. Serve along with White Chocolate Cosmopolitans.

Yield: about 15 servings

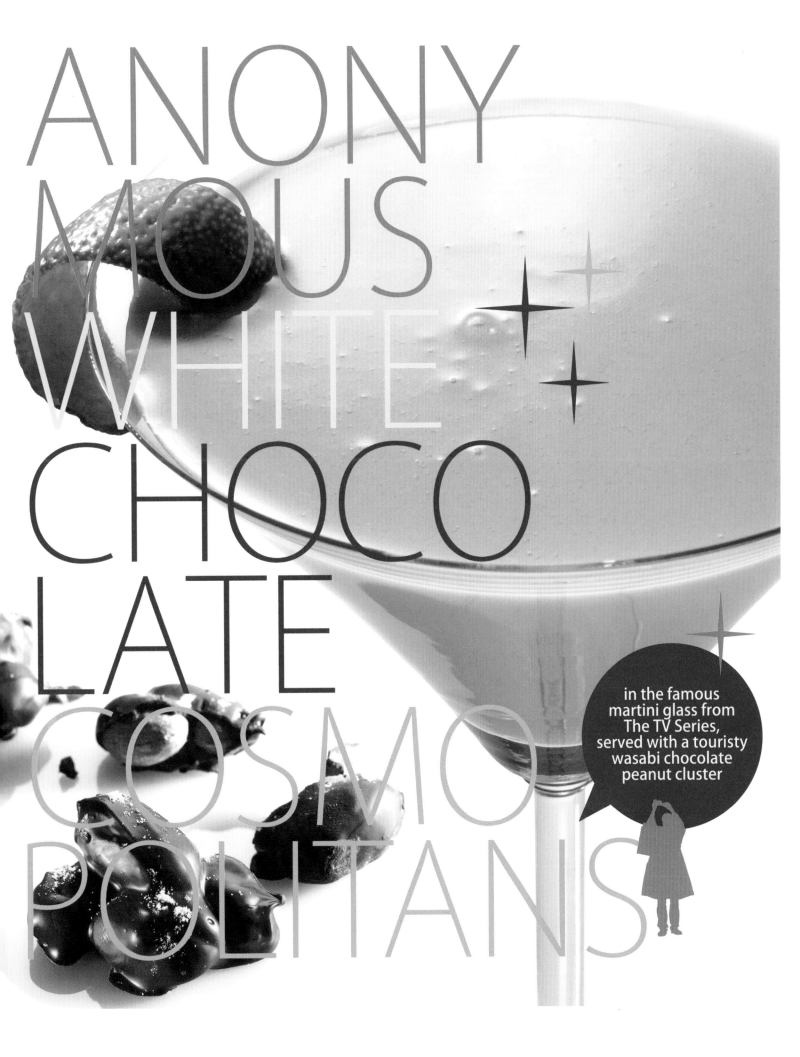

ANONY MOUS WHITE CHOCO LATE COSMO POLITANS

in the famous martini glass from The TV Series, served with a touristy wasabi chocolate peanut cluster

A Sugar Rush: Straightforward Chocolate Drinks, 141

Recipe 66

I got it from Sarah many years ago but I never tried it and never will, leaving it unbridled, renewing itself again and again in my imagination and dreams, for this recipe is the recipe of the passion that creates in me forever the desire to live.

Cake

2 sticks unsalted butter
½ cup unsweetened cocoa powder, sifted
1 cup water
2 cups all-purpose flour
2 cups granulated sugar
1 teaspoon baking soda
½ teaspoon salt
2 large eggs, lightly beaten
½ cup buttermilk
1 ½ teaspoons vanilla extract

Frosting

½ stick unsalted butter
¼ cup unsweetened cocoa powder
3 tablespoons buttermilk
2 cups confectioners' sugar
½ teaspoon vanilla extract
½ cup chopped walnuts

1. Make the cake. Preheat the oven to 375°F. Butter and flour a 9 by 13-inch cake pan.

2. Melt the butter in a medium saucepan. Whisk in the cocoa powder and water. Bring to a boil, then remove from the heat. Let cool.

3. In a large bowl, mix together the flour, granulated sugar, baking soda, and salt. Add the eggs, buttermilk, and vanilla. Blend well. Add the cocoa mixture, stirring until just combined. Pour the batter into the prepared pan. Bake until a toothpick inserted in the center comes out almost clean, 25 to 30 minutes.

4. Make the frosting. Melt the butter in a medium saucepan. Whisk in the cocoa powder and buttermilk. Bring to a boil, then remove from the heat.

5. Using a handheld mixer, beat the confectioners' sugar, vanilla, and walnuts into the cocoa mixture. Mix until thoroughly combined. Pour over the cooled cake.

Yield: 10 servings

Metric Conversions

Ounces to grams . . . . multiply ounces by 28.35
Pounds to grams . . . . multiply pounds by 453.5
Pounds to kilos . . . . multiply pounds by 0.45
Cups to liters . . . . multiply cups by 0.24
Fahrenheit to centigrade . . . . subtract 32 from Fahrenheit, multiply by 5, then divide by 9

Exact Equivalents

Weight:

1 ounce . . . . 28.35 grams
1 pound . . . . 453.59 grams

Volume:

1 cup . . . . . . 16 tablespoons / 8 fluid ounces / 236.6 milliliters
1 tablespoon . . . 3 teaspoons / 0.5 fluid ounce / 14.8 milliliters
1 teaspoon . . . . 4.9 milliliters
1 pint . . . . 2 cups / 473.2 milliliters

Approximate Metric Equivalents by Weight

¼ ounce . . . . 7 grams
½ ounce . . . . 14 grams
1 ounce . . . . 28 grams
1¼ ounces . . . . 35 grams
1½ ounces . . . . 40 grams
1⅔ ounces . . . . 45 grams
2 ounces . . . . 55 grams
2½ ounces . . . . 70 grams
4 ounces . . . . 112 grams
5 ounces . . . . 140 grams
8 ounces . . . . 228 grams
10 ounces . . . . 280 grams
15 ounces . . . . 425 grams
16 ounces (1 pound) . . . . 454 grams

Approximate Metric Equivalents by Volume

¼ cup . . . . 60 milliliters
⅓ cup . . . . 80 milliliters
½ cup . . . . 120 milliliters
⅔ cup . . . . 160 milliliters
1 cup . . . . 230 milliliters
1¼ cups . . . . 300 milliliters
1½ cups . . . . 360 milliliters

1⅔ cups . . . . 400 milliliters
2 cups . . . . 460 milliliters
2½ cups . . . . 600 milliliters
3 cups . . . . 700 milliliters
4 cups (quart) . . . . 0.95 liter
1.06 quarts . . . . 1 liter
4 quarts (1 gallon) . . . . 3.8 liters

Approximate Metric Equivalent by Temperature

100 degrees F . . . . 40 degrees C
200 degrees F . . . . 90 degrees C
250 degrees F . . . . 120 degrees C
300 degrees F . . . . 150 degrees C
325 degrees F . . . . 160 degrees C
350 degrees F . . . . 175 degrees C
375 degrees F . . . . 190 degrees C
400 degrees F . . . . 205 degrees C
425 degrees F . . . . 220 degrees C
450 degrees F . . . . 235 degrees C

Approximate Metric Equivalents by Length

⅛ inch . . . . 0.3 centimeter
¼ inch . . . . 0.6 centimeter
1 inch . . . . 2.5 centimeters
2 inches . . . . 5.08 centimeters
4 inches . . . . 10.16 centimeters
5 inches . . . . 13 centimeters
6 inches . . . . 15.24 centimeters
8 inches . . . . 20.32 centimeters
9 inches . . . . 22.86 centimeters
10 inches . . . . 25.4 centimeters
12 inches . . . . 30.48 centimeters
14 inches . . . . 35.56 centimeters
16 inches . . . . 40.64 centimeters
20 inches . . . . 50.8 centimeters

Helpful Equivalents

1 stick butter . . . . 100 grams
1 envelope gelatin . . . . 7 grams
1 envelope yeast . . . . 14.8 milliliters